En

M000033671

Practical. Insightful. Helpful. Biblical. Those are the standards by which I measure a book. And that's exactly what Mike and Rhonda Garrett deliver in *Love Needs*. I trust their wise counsel. I respect their marriage and the way they live their lives. ***Love Needs* will strengthen the best of marriages and will give hope and help to those who are struggling.** Congratulations! You've written a winner!

Dr. Henry Oursler, Founder, *Bringing Truth to Life,* President, *LeaderShape*

The Garrett's new book, *Love Needs*, is **an excellent guide to marital enrichment,** based on both biblical and clinical resources. It is written in a manner that is clear, concise, and wonderfully practical. I would highly commend it to couples and counselors."

Sam R. Williams, PhD, Professor of Counseling, Southeastern Baptist Theological Seminary, Wake Forest, NC

When we don't know where to begin to improve our marriage, Mike and Rhonda give us the practical, applicable, proven tools that they've used in counseling hundreds of couples so that we can immediately begin improving our communication and connection. We can almost hear them speaking with their compassionate wisdom as they would in their counseling office. They know we need fresh insight and more importantly, ways to apply it; so they've filled the book with practical action points. We often have the privilege of speaking on the topic of marriage, and we love having **a resource to share that can breathe new life into hurting couples.**

Tim and Joy Downs, Family Life Speaker Team, authors of *Fight Fair* and *One of Us Must Be Crazy and I'm Pretty Sure It's You!*

If you feel things could be better in your marriage but you can't put your finger on what they are, maybe there are blind spots in the way you relate to each other. The tools you need to accurately assess your relationship needs and fulfill them are now in this readable book. The practical insights and applications will bring to light what has previously been hidden. You may have several "Ah Ha!" moments, and the Action Points at the end of each chapter will help you know the next steps to take. This book will help guide you on **a workable path to a maximum marriage**. I have known Mike and Rhonda for over 25 years. They love to help couples and they live what they write about.

Dick Purnell, Cru Staff, author of sixteen Christian books

Love Needs by Mike and Rhonda Garrett, is a delightful 30 chapter devotional book aimed to help every couple discover their own love needs and re-think every aspect of their relationship so to 'upgrade' their marriage and love better. **Well written, easy to read, full of helpful steps** to meaningfully move one's marriage from 'just getting through the hectic day' to 'loving each other well and flourishing.' I recommend every couple take a 30 day challenge to read a chapter a day of 'Love Needs' and discover how to love each other better. In *Love Needs* the Garretts review the 30 love needs, and provide 30 small insights that if applied will have big impact on one's marriage."

Sharon May, PhD, Founder of Safe Haven Relationship Center, author of *Safe Haven Marriage* and *How To Argue so Your Spouse Will Listen*

"As a pastor and a licensed counselor, I am continuously on the lookout for new resources to help couples improve their relationship and to help me grow in my skills as a professional. In this one great book, Mike and Rhonda Garrett, have delivered both! **The church and the professional counseling community owe you a big "Thank** you". **What a great resource**. I love the simplicity of the assessment tool, and how the outcome becomes a road map to help guide your partner to meet these most important needs. Simple, Biblical, professional, and based on real world experience with thousands of couples. I love it and plan to use it in many ways!"

Anthony Thomas, LCSW, Executive Director
Marriage Menders & Family Counseling,
Discipleship Pastor, Crossroads Fellowship, Raleigh, NC

In *Love Needs*, the Garretts offer couples numerous categories to help them pinpoint and name areas which they long to share with their partners to be successful in communicating and getting needs met. One question they recommend asking is, "Do you need a solution or support?" This question can help ensure that partners don't miss each other as they try to communicate. There are many such **useful tools offered to those who long for more** in their precious marriage. It is a helpful tool for improving relationships.

Sue Richards, MACP, LPCA, counselor, teacher, author

Rarely do you find a book that targets the specific, practical skills and attitudes that actually make a marriage work. *Love Needs* is **a spectacular set of tools, wisely applied, that will help any husband and wife** make a difficult marriage better….or a good marriage great. The Garretts have helped countless couples improve their marriage—and their best insights are captured in this book!

Paula Rinehart, LCSW, therapist, teacher, author of *Strong Women, Soft Hearts* and *Sex and the Soul of a Woman*

LOVE NEEDS

LOVE NEEDS

DISCOVER YOUR TOP 10 LANGUAGES OF LOVING

Mike Garrett Ph.D., L.P.C.

Rhonda Garrett M.A., L.P.C.

LOVE NEEDS: Discover Your Top 10 Languages of Loving

Copyright © 2019

by Mike Garrett, Ph.D. and Rhonda Garrett, M.A.

Published in the United States of America by Kindle Direct Publishing.

All rights reserved. No portion of this book may be reproduced, stored in a retrieval system, or transmitted in any form or by any means—electronic, mechanical, photocopy, recording, scanning or any other—except for brief quotations in critical reviews or articles, without the prior written permission of one of the authors.

Unless otherwise noted, Scripture quotations are taken from the THE HOLY BIBLE, English Standard Version® (ESV®), copyright 2001 by Crossway, a publishing ministry of Good News Publishers. Used by permission. All rights reserved.

ISBN: 9781792693632

Imprint: Independently published

To our three daughters: Julie, Jessica and Jenny

We love you more than we can express. There is no greater joy than to see you walk in truth.

To our grandchildren: Ethan, Annie, Caleb, Rachel and Zachary

You are loved and covered in prayer.

How To Use This Book

1. Take the Love Needs assessment at the back of this book to identify your top relational needs at this present time. This is not a report card to show failures but more of a wish list of what makes you feel loved. Invite your partner to also take the assessment separately.

2. Place a check mark by your ten (10) highest scores and rank those "Top 10 Love Needs" in order of priority. This is your personal love list of how you want to be treated.

3. Review your lists together and explain what each of your "Top 10 Love Needs" looks like. Give specific examples.

4. Read each of your specific "Top 10 Love Needs" chapters in the book separately and together in order to expand your discussion and give further ideas and suggestions.

5. Transfer your "Top 10 Love Needs" to a card and trade cards with your spouse for immediate application. Make this newly requested list your daily intentional focus for at least one month. Have fun!

LOVE NEEDS

CONTENTS

LOVE NEEDS

Introduction

Blaise Pascal, the renowned seventeenth century French philosopher, mathematician, scientist and theologian stated, "There is a God-shaped vacuum in the heart of each man which cannot be satisfied by any created thing but only by God the Creator, made known through Jesus Christ." [1] In other words, our deepest desires are met in a personal relationship with the true and living God. We believe that. We also believe that many interpersonal love needs can be met through interpersonal relationships when they are clarified and communicated.

White collars, blue collars, gold collars and no collars . . . all shapes and sizes seem to find their way into our counseling offices. We lead a team of dedicated Licensed Professional Counselors in Raleigh, North Carolina and have regularly counseled young and old, husbands, wives, singles, youth and children. Our clients have included rich and poor, employed and unemployed, Christians and non-Christians, salesmen, musicians, ship captains, entertainers, native American Indian chiefs, race car drivers, college students, coaches, pastors, politicians, psychiatrists, mechanics, business professionals, doctors, lawyers, teachers, art curators, web-designers, IT specialists, therapists, pilots and an amazing variety of others. *They all seem to be looking for love*. Many have found this love from above but still regularly report a great frustration when other needs are not being met by their significant other. Sometimes the disappointment is with a parent but usually it is with the spouse who is coming up short and misunderstanding love needs.

We believe that both Blaise Paschal and many of our clients are right. Our supreme love need is a personal relationship with our Creator Lord and Savior Jesus Christ. And that relationship is a free gift that provides eternal life and forgiveness of sins to all who will "believe and receive" (see John 1:12). Having said that, let's look at how this plays out in interpersonal human relationships. A faith relationship with the Lord will meet the deepest needs of our heart. But we still find ourselves with love needs at a human level. That's what this book is all about.

30 Languages of Loving

"How do I love thee? Let me count the ways."[2] Can they be counted on one hand, or two hands, or ten fingers and toes? Or are there even more? And could it be that the list might even grow? We assessed several thousand couples in classes and counseling sessions over a ten-year period (2008-2018). We have documented at least 30 distinct and recurring ways of giving and receiving love within a marriage relationship and have seen patterns emerge that led to the "Love Needs Assessment" at the end of this book. We also regularly counsel more than 40 couples every week and continue to validate and improve our findings. Our "Love Needs Assessment" has now been used, studied and modified for many years in a private practice setting by our team of licensed therapists before releasing it to the public. This material is not based on fanciful guesswork but on continual couple assessments completed in the trenches of relationship interviews within a conscientious therapeutic setting.

Relationship 2.0

What does "better" look like? What is the bull's eye for a better and lasting relationship? We often see couples in our private practice that seem to be dragging along with a "Relationship 1.0 is good enough" mentality. It is an easy rut to fall into. But we encourage our couples to consider upgrading the quality of their relationship and clarifying specific ways to give and receive love to each other. We upgrade our cell phones. We upgrade our computers. We upgrade our memberships. We upgrade careers. We upgrade travel plans. Maybe it's time to upgrade your foremost human relationship . . . your marriage.

Words of Encouragement

The Love Needs Assessment (at the back of this book) is not a short term exercise only. It is a starting point for the long-term marathon of upgrading your relationship. This is about bringing love to the next level and about continuing to "bring it." This is a 30-minute screening that could influence the next 30 years of meaningful connection. Many of our clients come to counseling because they are feeling stifled with not knowing how to make their partner happy. Many have even stated they are not even sure what their own languages of loving are. This time-tested Love Needs checklist has proven to be the way out of the ditch of disconnection for many couples. Take this assessment carefully and prayerfully. Don't file this away and forget it. Turn this into a permanent relationship transformer. Emblazon it on your heart and soul as you share the results back and forth with your spouse. We even give our couples the assignment of taking the Love Needs Assessment and then recording their "Top 10 Love Needs" on an index card to keep in their wallet or handbag. We then encourage them to prayerfully review this card for at least 30 days, often asking themselves, "Which of these ways can I show love to my spouse today?" Life-change and increased love is inevitable.

Denial or Demand

This assessment is about acknowledging desires instead of promoting demands. On the road to a quality

relationship there are two ditches, one on either side—
denying that needs exist and *demanding* that needs be
met. Beware of both.

The Ditch of Denial

Some people deny that they have desires. The message
playing in their head goes something like this, "I
shouldn't expect to be loved. I should only think of
others. Shame on me for having wishes and wants."
That message is often reinforced by many external
voices insisting that all one's attention be focused
externally.

Sometimes it is an internal, recurring audio of voices
from the past. It often originates from a family of origin
dysfunction that shames and guilt-trips all participants
who express feelings or personal preferences. The
embedded message is that you must accommodate
others even to the point of enabling unhealthy
behaviors. These unhealthy behaviors are usually
exhibited by one or more dominant persons within the
family structure.

Sometimes the voice comes from an internal,
unbalanced religious loudspeaker condemning all
thoughts of care and concern for self. Self needs and
desires are considered *selfish* and *evil* intentions and
need to be extinguished. For instance, John 12:24
states, "Unless a grain of wheat falls into the earth and
dies, it remains alone; but if it dies, it bears much fruit."

Therefore the biblical concept of "death to self" can be misused and inappropriately exalted at the expense of other balancing scriptures. Overemphasized truth becomes heresy. In this case then, it is falsely assumed that there can be no thought of self-worth, value or personal considerations as taught in other scripture (Matt. 19:19; Matt. 22:39; Mark 12:31; Phil 2:4).

The net result of all this pre-programming is the denial of any legitimate human wishes, wants and desires. In this ditch of denial you will be seduced by approval addiction in order to keep a sense of stability in your environment. And you will robotically live for others but miss out on at least half of the basic human quest that is "to love and *be loved*." The antidote for living in the ditch of denial is to practice calm assertiveness regarding your own needs while also considering the needs of others.

The Ditch of Demandingness

On the other side of the road to a quality relationship is the "ditch of demandingness." Self-assertiveness carried to an extreme becomes the heresy of demandingness and the recipe for relationship trouble. Demandingness says, "My way is right and your way doesn't matter." There is no collaboration in the self-absorbed, navel-gazing selfishness of a "my way or the highway" mentality in relationships. People often get two wheels off the road into the ditch of demandingness for several reasons.

Sometimes demandingness is a cry for love and value because of unmet needs in the childhood family or in other previous adult relationships.

Sometimes it is a personality trait of a dominant "Type A" who is accustomed to controlling others and occupying the spotlight.

Sometimes demandingness comes from keeping score. In other words, "If you haven't shown concern for my needs then why should I show concern for yours?" Inevitably, the ditch of demandingness fuels narcissism in the life of the dominant partner and can create deep pain and loss of identity in the other partner. Demandingness can easily lead to verbal, emotional or physical abuse

The Solution

Keep it between the ditches. First, stay away from that ditch of denial. And secondly, don't get your wheels off into the trench of dominating demandingness. Admit that you are human and that you have needs. Understand yourself and your deepest longings. Be gently vocal in expressing your personal wishes, wants, needs and desires. Be willing to express and request your desires and yet hold them with an open hand and not a closed fist of forceful ultimatums. Lower your expectations. And above all, consider one another with love and grace.

Consider Others

After communicating your needs, resolve with your spouse to join the ranks of master marriages in which each partner shifts the focus from "my needs" to "your needs." In the healthiest relationships, partners consider each other as equal or greater in value and the needs of the other as more important as well (see Philippians 2:2-5). When both partners catch sight of this vision and get on the love train of giving and not just receiving, then a deeper level of connectedness and emotional closeness begins to unfold in the marriage.

CHAPTER 1

LOVE NEED #1: WORKING ON OUR RELATIONSHIP

"Enjoy life with your wife . . ."　　Ecclesiastes 9:9 NIV

A most ambitious examination of one of America's largest demographic, the millennial generation (those born approximately 1980-2000), was conducted by the Pew Research Center, a nonpartisan fact tank. A study of 2,020 individuals found that this demographic values relationships. The survey concluded, "Millennials (like the older boomer generation) place parenthood and marriage far above career and financial success." [1]

In all of our many years of working with couples we never heard anyone come close to saying, "We hope to find the right person, fall hopelessly and passionately in love, have a beautiful wedding, live together for a while then let our relationship disintegrate and crash and burn in divorce." The conversation usually goes something like this: "We can't wait to get married and live happily ever after." And imbedded in that dream is the idea of forever and ever.

So if finding, building and growing a permanent relationship bond is the aim of most couples, why is it that so many of these dreams and dreamers get frustrated? Lack of attention to proper priorities is often the culprit. We have discovered that marital drift can happen to the best of couples. More couples drift apart than blow apart. Negative drift is often the result of well-meaning focus on some really good things like careers and children. Then, if you throw in unhealthy individual problems or everyday distractions, then the drift accelerates. Even couples that do a great job of balancing work and family find themselves drifting away from marital oneness. After a few years they find themselves miles apart but still sharing the same address and bedroom (sometimes). We often hear couples in their 50's stating, "The kids will soon be gone and we don't know if we will make it. Can you help us?"

Couples must discuss how to love and be loved to maintain the priority of the marriage dyad. Plan A should always be, ". . . they shall *become* (italics ours) one" (Genesis 2:24). Wonderful oneness with the Creator and with our life partner has always been God's remedy for aloneness. But "become" is the operative word in that succinct challenge. It doesn't just happen. It takes continual intentional "becoming" effort, especially in the love needs each spouse, for the bond of love to grow. Every day is a new opportunity for "becoming" and experiencing attachment connectedness. And that is a "oneness" that is more than physical or sexual. Oneness involves the total person. Oneness in marriage is to be an emotional bond, a spiritual bond and a physical bond. Each spouse must make the relationship a priority and then focus on each other's love needs in order for oneness to become a reality.

In order to maintain the priority of the relationship there must be an ongoing evaluation and balancing of the "me" and the "we" times experienced. Before marriage, decisions can be made primarily around "me." Constant consideration of another person isn't usually necessary. But a committed couple needs to think in terms of pleasing the other person and insuring there are designated "we" times together. Our mantra for couples goes like this: "Schedule *Daily* talk times, *Weekly* dates, *Monthly* extended times and *Quarterly* Retreats." We say it over and over on a regular basis. "We" need regular undistracted devoted couple time and that must be scheduled or marital drift is inevitable.

Action Points:

- Renew your commitment to each other to make your relationship a priority over other relationships, work or other involvements. Discuss what that will look like practically.
- Schedule *Daily* talk times, *Weekly* dates, *Monthly* extended times and *Quarterly* retreats.☺

CHAPTER 2

LOVE NEED #2: EMOTIONAL CLOSENESS

"When a man is newly married . . . he shall be free at home one year to be happy with his wife whom he has taken." Deuteronomy 24:5

E vidence-based studies have shown that "couples who perceived their spouses to be emotionally available, accessible, and responsive reported having happier and healthier marriages."[1] One researcher, Dr. John Gottman, studied over 3000 couples and found that couples who accept each other's "bids for connection" were much more likely to stay happily married through the seasons of life.[2] The key to the success and longevity of marriages is not *if* couples have conflict but rather *how* couples communicate and connect and how couples manage inevitable conflict.

The crucial factors for building and maintaining emotional closeness have been proven to be threefold in our experience. First, there must be regularly scheduled as well as spontaneous times devoted to "heart talk." Couples need to make their relationship connection through communication a top priority. We define "heart talk" as undistracted devoted couple communication time. Devices need to be turned off. All media needs to be shut down and focus needs to be centered on each other. Finding a quiet , undistracted place is supremely important. So sending the kids to play in another room essential. Perhaps getting out of the house for a twenty-minute walk will work if the children are old enough to be left alone and cooperate. The time must be spent with an attitude of considering the other person and not correcting or attacking.

First, we recommend that a great place to start is to talk about the daily ups and downs of life or the hopes and dreams of each partner. We refer to these as the Wows, Wishes, Worries and Wounds. This allows each spouse into the world of the other's heart and soul. The time may be spent talking, listening, asking questions, clarifying, praying and just understanding and accepting each other. Offering more *support* than *solution* is key. If a partner is going through a problem it is always good to ask, "Do you need solution or support." And the answer will usually be, "support!" For more ideas see our Chapter 10 (Quality Communication).

Secondly, couples must practice *accepting invitations to intimacy*. Intimacy is always based on emotional and relational connection as the foundation for a quality physical or sexual union. We hear spouses in our office almost daily explain, "I don't feel like sex if I don't feel close to you." Throughout each day partners are giving off direct and sometime subtle invitations to enter into each other's world. Learning to pick up on these invitations is a skill that needs daily sharpening. Sometimes these invitations come in the form of a statement, idea, joke or interest. But they are basically a gesture of reaching out, wanting the other person to engage and participate. Acknowledging the invitation with sensitive responsiveness and willing participation is a small but foundational part of daily bridge-building experienced by master marriages.

Thirdly, there must be substantial repair attempts done effectively *when* and not *if* conflicts arise. There is a skill we discuss in chapter 5 (Repaired Hurts) about conflict management that transforms conflict into connection. To summarize, it first involves reducing escalation by calling time-out and rescheduling. Then after self-care and self-soothing (and not reloading) the wounded partner needs to calmly return with the sole intent of expressing their hurt feelings hoping to gain a sensitive audience. When the offending partner learns to receive this information non-defensively and respond with understanding, empathy and apology, relational connection is transformed.

Action Points:

- Discuss "heart talk" in Love Need # 10: Quality Communication.
- Discuss what your daily "invitations to intimacy" look like.
- Read and discuss Love Need #5: Repaired Hurts.

LOVE NEEDS

CHAPTER 3

LOVE NEED #3: SEXUAL INTIMACY

". . . the two shall become one . . ."   Ephesians 5:31

Sex is God's idea! He thought it up and He created male and female with the plan that the two shall become one. He even placed a book called *Song of Solomon* right smack dab in the middle of the Bible to reveal his incredibly bold endorsement of emotional, physical and sexual love between a man and a woman. And if *Song of Solomon* doesn't light your fire then you've got wet wood!

The problem, unfortunately, in many relationships is that there is a mismatch when it comes to sexual desire. Men will most often (but not always) have a much higher libido and desire greater frequency of sex. They consistently report that they feel closer to their partner if they are having regular sexual relationship. Their mindset is most often, "Give me sex so I can feel close to you." Usually the woman is seeking greater emotional connection and wishing the guy was pursuing and cherishing her as a person and not just wanting her body. It is not uncommon to hear a woman say something to the effect, "I don't want sex because he treats me so badly." Her mindset is, "I need to feel close to you and then I might be open to having sex with you." She needs to feel loved and valued to even consider the act of intimacy.

Occasionally there will be a role reversal and the woman is the one desiring more physical intimacy. This is true with 10-20% of the couples we counsel. Sometimes it is not so much a higher sex drive as it is a greater desire for intimacy overall and sex just becomes the focus. So let's talk about how to alleviate mismatches, especially in the sexual relationship. Regardless of which partner is expressing the greater need for physical and sexual intimacy, there seems to be one alternative that is helpful.

This recommendation may seem counterintuitive. Most of the time the partner with the higher sex drive spends far too much energy trying to get the resistant spouse to come up to their level of interest. In other words," If you will only start thinking, acting and feeling the way I do then we will be OK." Unfortunately, it never seems to work that way. Sometimes they can get some short term efforts out of the less interested partner but those efforts are difficult to sustain. A much more productive strategy is for the person with the higher sex drive to be willing to come down to a more agreeable frequency of sexual intimacy. Then, if the person who has the lesser interest is willing to consistently step up their initiation and cooperation, most couples are able to meet somewhere in the middle. This mismatch dilemma is therefore minimized if not resolved. Each couple needs to find the middle ground that works for both partners.

Love-mapping is another skill that helps couples find a mutually satisfying, happy place in their love life. Love-mapping is an exercise that needs to be completed by both partners individually and then a time is needed to collaborate together. We have couples think through and write down their preferences around six stages of lovemaking (see below). Most couples affirm that they talked about these issues early in the relationship but then stopped talking much about sex. Noted sex researcher Shere Hite, in the only book about sex that has sold over 50 million copies, found that women especially wished they could just talk to their partner about what they wanted.[1] Imagine that! Talking will help your overall relationship. So make time at least annually to talk about your love-maps.

Action Points: Discuss each of the following stages of lovemaking.
- **Attitude:** What is the overall perspective you desire regarding sexual intimacy?
- **Atmosphere:** How do you want to be treated all week leading up to lovemaking?
- **Approach:** What would help you be in the mood on the day of lovemaking?
- **Arousal:** What do you like and dislike during foreplay? Be specific.
- **Apex:** Describe your dream ending to intercourse?
- **Afterglow:** How do you like to be treated afterwards (that evening and the next day)?

LOVE NEEDS

CHAPTER 4

LOVE NEED #4: PHYSICAL CONNECTION

"Anyone who goes too far alone . . . goes mad."
Jewish Proverb

J ohn plopped down on our couch next to his sweetheart and opened up the personal assessment that he had meticulously labored over. It was the first time this struggling couple had identified their "Top 10 Love Needs." At the top of his list was "Physical Connection." Further down the list was "Sexual Intimacy." His bride of many years sat focused with eye-popping curiosity as he explained the difference. It was non-sexual physical touch that made him feel most loved!

Touch can be stronger than verbal or emotional interaction. In one modern study 73 mothers were asked to provide skin-to-skin contact daily for one hour to their prematurely born infants for 14 consecutive days.[1] They were compared to 73 premature infants who received standard incubator care. These mother-infant dyads were then evaluated seven times across the first ten years of life. The study found that mothers in the physical contact group were more sensitive and expressed more maternal nurturing behaviors toward their infants than the mothers of babies in the incubator group. Children in the physical contact group showed better cognitive skills and executive abilities in repeated testing from six months to ten years, than the other children did. At ten years the children who had received physical contact showed more organized sleep, better neuroendocrine response to stress, more mature functioning of the autonomic nervous system and better cognitive control. The enhanced level of physical stimulation positively influenced the development of the brain and deepened the relationship between mother and child.

Touch is critical for children's growth, development and health. This also seems to be true for adults' physical, mental and relational well-being. In today's world of ever-increasing online relationships we are becoming dangerously touch-deprived and creating in ourselves a touch-hunger due to a shortage of tactile stimulation. Touching, holding hands, putting arms around each other, bumping, leaning toward and wanting to embrace are essential features of this interpersonal phenomenon. Often one partner is much more the initiator and the other responding partner shows varying degrees of receptivity and reciprocal activity. It is important to recognize that the more physical partner is reaching for connection and sending invitations to intimacy at a certain level. Everything isn't always about sex! Often the more touchy-feely person simply wants to experience an atmosphere of acceptance and connection. They need to know that they are in a safe and secure zone of a caring relationship. They are reaching out in hopes that they will be received and valued. It is often a subconscious, instinctive way of functioning. It says, "I like you and I want to be friends." It says, "You mean a lot, if not the world, to me." It says, "I am comfortable being with you and I enjoy your company." It says, "I want to love and to be loved."

Close proximity is also an integral part of this language of loving. A partner who wants to touch and snuggle up is usually a partner who likes close proximity. Why sit on opposite sides of the room when you can sit beside each other? Why walk by each other without touching in some flirty way? Why leave for work without making a point of embracing and engaging in some sort of bodily contact? And why not kiss when you give out hugs? It all makes sense to the physical person. Sometimes it translates into sitting beside each other in restaurants instead of sitting opposite each other at the table or booth. And there may be an occasional pat-pat-pat on the couch that says, "Come sit by me . . . close proximity please." At least that is what happens in our house!

Action Points:

- Discuss what kind of touching is appreciated .
- Discuss what kind of touching is not appreciated.
- Discuss what response is desired with the touching.
- Discuss whether touching should lead to sex.

LOVE NEEDS

CHAPTER 5

LOVE NEED #5: REPAIRED HURTS

"Forgive us our trash baskets as we forgive those who pass trash against us."   Anonymous 1st Grader

You can't go forward until you go back. That is a principle we have learned the hard way. So many couples enter into counseling with at least one partner focused on moving forward and assuring the other partner there is no need to talk about past mistakes or conflicts. "I already apologized so there is no use picking at an old sore" was the proclamation of one partner sitting on our couch. This sounds logical on the surface. But the problem is that old relationship wounds have contributed to a broader *attachment injury* that the couple will not be able to ignore without several substantial repair attempts.

We find it highly beneficial to interview a couple and draw out a timeline of their relationship history. We hear each person's version separately and draw a graph of the highs and lows (0-100% satisfaction) over all the years they have been together. Frequently a time is reported when the couple connection dropped down nearly to the zero range. We refer to that period as the "I'm done" days. Some couples remember a brief time like that. Others report repeated events and themes in their relationship that took them way beyond the "three strikes and you're out" position. It is not uncommon to see distressed couples report recurring patterns of hurt and/or betrayal. When we propose a "repair attempt" conversation in our office couples consistently nod in agreement that they know this needs to take place . . . even if they have already tried to do this on their own.

What is a "repair attempt" conversation? First of all, let's address what it is not. It is not a time to hurl attacks on the offending partner and harp on all the wrongs they have done. That usually has already happened! Rather, it is a time to focus primarily on the hurts and pains that have been the experience of the offended party. And it is vital that only one person tries to share their hurts in this conversation. We always start with whoever was hurt *first* of *worse*. And specifically the conversation is to be centered on the painful soft emotions (e.g. unloved, unvalued, abandoned, betrayed, disrespected, etc.) that have been felt by the "wounded" partner.

The focus of this time needs to be the wounded partner sharing all the painful emotions they have experienced. But the hurts should be in connection to *only one* painful event or theme (an ongoing negative pattern) at this time. This will only work if the wounded partner explains his own emotions and does not criticize the other with "you" statements.

The listening partner, whom we refer to as the

"repairer," needs to write down every feeling/emotion word and every need his partner presents. This will allow him to respond, not with defensiveness or debate but only with empathy and compassion. The repairer should "follow the feelings" and only explore the written hurt feelings and needs. The repairer must stay on track to give four consecutive responses (see below).

Action Points:

1. **Understand:** Ask about each of the painful emotions. Say, "Explain that emotion. Please unpack that emotion. Help me understand better what that did to you." And then explore the explanation, continuing to "follow the feelings."
2. **Empathize:** The wounded person needs to know that the repairer really "gets it" and "feels it." The repairer needs to express true feelings of sadness and regret over the pain expressed.
3. **Apologize:** After there is increased understanding and empathy it is time to apologize again, but this time more fully. The apology needs to be not only about what happened but also about the pain that was caused.
4. **Change:** After the repairer has completed the first three steps, discuss the new relationship agreements that can be collaborated in order to avoid repeated grievances.

LOVE NEEDS

CHAPTER 6

LOVE NEED #6: RESPECT AND APPRECIATION

". . . if there is anything worthy of praise, think about these things." Philippians 4:8

E verybody likes to be respected and appreciated . . . some more than others. Nobody enjoys being disrespected or unappreciated. An exercise we have found to be most helpful is to do an in-depth analysis of the couple's conflict pattern. We refer to this as their "Conflict Cycle." It never fails that one or the other partner reports that feeling a lack of respect or appreciation. The offending partner usually says they can't help disrespecting the other due because of the hurts and wounds they are feeling in the relationship. In other words, "I can't help reacting and keeping score! And besides, what goes around comes around."

One author dubs this pattern as the "crazy cycle." His explanation goes like this: "Without love, she reacts without respect. Without respect, he reacts without love—ad nauseam."[2] So we try to help couples become more aware of this rigid, negative and circular pattern with the goal of trying to reduce the negative interactions and increase the positive interactions.

Does it ever feel like your partner only criticizes? Can you even remember the last time your partner said something encouraging? When negative interactions outweigh the positive ones it may be difficult to recall the good qualities in your partner. Successful and stable relationships keep a focus on positive rather than negative words and behaviors. "The ratio of positive to negative interactions in stable relationships is 5:1 not 0.8:1 as it is in couples headed for divorce." [3]

The truly successful relationships that we might call "master marriages" actually score more in the 14:1 range. This means that for every one negative interaction between partners there should be at least five positive interactions. And fourteen positives would be preferred. Partners create damage in the relationship when they criticize, give constant negative feedback, are not supportive, withhold affection, show dismissive disinterest, and lack respectful appreciation.

How would one go about increasing the positives and showing more respect and appreciation? It involves emotional attunement and consideration of the wishes, wants, needs and desires of your partner. And it means doing marriage by the Golden Rule: "Do unto others as you would have them do unto you" (Matthew 7:12). Some refer to a platinum rule: "Do unto others the way *they* would have you do unto *them*." It also involves being intentional to remember and affirm the positive qualities of your partner on a regular basis. Even though you could "catch them doing something bad," make it a point to "catch them doing something good." Notice and compliment them when they are at their best instead of criticizing them when they are at their worst.

"Love covers a multitude of sins" (1 Peter 4:8). Keep the focus on what you like about your partner instead of what you don't like about them. Instead of worrying about them loving you, focus on giving them something of yourself that is worth loving. Cheerleaders are encouraging and so are thankful partners who maintain a positive perspective. Practicing praise and appreciation is vital to a healthy relationship and is always attractive to the other partner.

Action Points:

- List an "appreciation checklist" on a card you can carry. Practice the power of praise for one month toward your partner.
- Start a "Praise Journal" (a two-column sheet on the refrigerator) and for one month keep writing daily praises of each other.
- Write out and review the following exhortations: "Let *NO* corrupt talk come out of your mouths, but *ONLY* such as is good for building up" (Ephesians 4:29). ". . . whatever is lovely, whatever is commendable, if there is any excellence, if there is anything worthy of *praise*, think about these things" (Phil. 4:8).

CHAPTER 7

LOVE NEED #7: SERVANT LEADER

"Life is an exciting business, and it is most exciting when it is lived for others."   Helen Keller

I n New York City's Central Park stands a popular tourist attraction -- a bronze statue of "Balto the Wonder Dog." Balto was the lead Siberian husky of Iditarod sled musher Gunner Kaasen who is credited with saving the town of Nome, Alaska from a deadly diphtheria epidemic on February 2, 1925. Kaasen and Balto ran the last two legs of a multi-sled effort, racing against time from Anchorage, Alaska to Nome to deliver the life-saving antitoxin serum. Their part was the last 53 miles in blizzard conditions, chest deep snow drifts, wind chills below -40 degrees Fahrenheit and total white out conditions.

World-wide media coverage made Balto a common household name for an entire generation. The inscription on the New York statue reads, "Dedicated to the indomitable spirit of the sled dogs that relayed antitoxin 600 miles over rough ice, across treacherous waters, through arctic blizzards, from Nenana to the relief of stricken Nome." Balto was a super-hero servant leader. We need some Baltos today in relationships.

Wives commonly make the request of husbands, "I wish you would lead but I wish you would consider me and the kids more." Sounds like a call for Balto, doesn't it? The Bible instructs a man to "manage (*grk.* proistemi) his own family well" (1 Timothy 3:4). The meaning of that original Greek word seems to get lost in the translation. It actually means "to stand before or put oneself at the lead or out front."[1] Like the lead dog who takes the brunt of the elements, a husband should shield his family from the blizzard-like problems of life as much as possible.

Another interesting scriptural exhortation for the partnership (and especially for the man) is the idea that each person is to "*provide* for his relatives and especially for his immediate family" (1 Timothy 5:8). The Greek word for *provide* (pronoeo) actually means to "think ahead" and generally means to take care of someone by planning ahead for them. The same idea is demonstrated in the familiar story of the "good Samaritan" who "took care" (Luke 10:34) of someone in need. The primary idea is that we are to think ahead and plan ahead for the welfare of our spouse and family, first and foremost.

Many times in teaching marriage seminars we would teach the above concepts and then ask the women in the group a question, asking for a physical response. The question was, "How many of you women would like a husband who is taking a stand out in front of the family, thinking and planning ahead for you and the children?" Instead of a show of hands we would ask them to just nod up and down for *Yes* or left to right for *No*. Inevitably, every woman in every conference clearly nodded up and down with an "absolutely, that's what I'm talking about" grin on her face. It always brought a chuckle and energy to every group and clearly proved that servant leaders are desired in every partnership. We all like it when someone looks out for us, thinks ahead for us, and is committed to making our best interests a priority. That is Balto-style servant-leadership.

Action Points:

- Discuss with your partner ways you could each step out in front to think and plan ahead (e.g. finances, insurance, parenting, retirement, personal needs, etc.). Collaborate new agreements.
- Schedule a series of husband-wife business meetings to follow-up on this first discussion.
- Read and discuss Love Need # 14: Shared Decision-Making.

CHAPTER 8

LOVE NEED #8: DEFINED ROLES AND RESPONSIBILITIES

"For it is in giving that we receive."
St. Francis of Assisi

John and Sarah had only been married a few years but they seemed to be upside down in a ditch as they explained their struggle in our office. Sarah began by saying, "He expects me to do everything. He's never around to help me with anything." John's familiar retort went something like, "Somebody's got to work for a living. I have a hard job and I come home tired." Sarah's immediate reaction was, "Well, I have a job too, and then I come home and have to take care of the kids, the meals and everything else. I wish you would notice and be willing to do something instead of just disappearing." Then, as would be expected, John began to list all of his many contributions that she was not noticing. That's when Sarah's tears started to flow.

And so go many counseling sessions for couples who have not clearly defined their roles and responsibilities. There needs to be an agreed upon plan for division of labor in every home and it needs to be reviewed and updated periodically. It will essentially eliminate this ongoing battle of who is doing what and when. But it must be collaborated and the agreements must be followed consistently.

How does a couple define and delineate their roles and responsibilities? We recommend that you work on the following exercise separately and then plan a couple of sessions together to negotiate a new agreed upon "Future Roles and Responsibilities."

ACTION POINTS:

Use the exercise that follows. On your own, review and update all the jobs and routines that take place around your home and relationship (e.g., lawn, groceries, cooking, etc.). Once you have constructed this list then map out the "Present Roles and Responsibilities." Then use the last matrix "Future Roles and Responsibilities" to reassign responsibilities as you would desire. After you have worked on this exercise separately, spend time together considering what your partner is requesting. Collaborate to find a mutually satisfactory future plan. Make sure you are also agreeing on the timing for each action. And all the items addressed need to be on both of your calendars or conflict is inevitable. Once you reach a suitable agreement, post the final plan (i.e., on the fridge or pantry door) and call this a one month experiment. You can always come back and tweak your agreement.

STEP 1. UPDATE **RESPONSIBILITIES** LIST

Auto repair	Groceries	Meal Prep	Dishes
Fun stuff	Decorating	Planning	Housework
Investments	Intimacy	Romance	Setting Goals
Vacations	Talk times	Family fun	Dates
In-laws	Maintenance	Carpool	Daycare
Childcare	Bill paying	Church	Homework
Parenting	Entertaining	Checkbook	Retirement
Leisure	Yard Work	Spiritual Life	Exercise

Other 1_____   Other 2_____
Other 3_____   Other 4_____

STEP 2. LIST **PRESENT** ROLES & RESPONSIBILITIES

HUSBAND ONLY	HUSBAND WITH WIFE SUPPORT	BOTH TOGETHER	WIFE WITH HUSBAND SUPPORT	WIFE ONLY
ex. auto				

STEP 3. LIST **FUTURE** ROLES & RESPONSIBILITIES

HUSBAND ONLY	HUSBAND WITH WIFE SUPPORT	BOTH TOGETHER	WIFE WITH HUSBAND SUPPORT	WIFE ONLY

CHAPTER 9

LOVE NEED #9: SUPPORT OF MY DESIRE TO HELP OTHERS

"Only a life lived for others is worth living."
Albert Einstein

Rick was a single guy who liked helping people. He ran a rather large and quite successful family thrift store where people bought and sold used furniture and clothing. He made it a point to do business by the Golden Rule always trying to "do unto others as you would have them do unto you" (Matthew 7:12). Many of the workers he hired were people who were down on their luck. Quite a few of his best employees had come out of rehab programs and could not find anyone who would give them a second chance in life. But Rick did. Rick bought a truck and trailer, not so much for his vocation but more for his avocation. He liked helping folks in need in his church and community. Many Saturdays he would load up some used furniture and joyfully deliver it to some needy single parent or unemployed couple who couldn't even afford his discounted prices. Great is his reward in heaven!

The right girl will come along some day for Rick. But when she does it will be of paramount importance that she values and supports his desire to help others.

Rick will also need to modify his busy lifestyle of serving others to make sure his new partner becomes an even higher priority. He may even find great fulfillment in helping her find and fulfill her personal sense of gifting and calling. Ideally, he and his future companion will want to embrace each other's personal mission as well as advancing their individual life dreams. If only it would work that way for the many couples we see in counseling.

Quite often there is a conflict pattern going on in a relationship that centers around this issue. One partner feels called to do a great work of caring for others and meanwhile their spouse feels cheated. Each person is being offended by the other. One feels unloved and unimportant. The other feels unloved and criticized. Polarization begins because the more the first person leaves to go help others, the more the second person feels compelled to point out the error of their mistaken priorities. Conversely, the more the second person attempts to stop their own pain by pulling their partner back, the more the first person pulls to justify and continue their high and holy calling to serve.

So what should be done to remedy this conflict pattern? A truce has to be called. Then there needs to be a renewed effort to work together on an acceptable vision, calling, passion and mission for each individual that aligns with mutual couple goals. There also needs to be renewed commitment to keeping balanced with a focus on the couple bond. There must be dedication to both quantity and quality of time together. Often when a couple determines to lay down arms and put their relationship back at the forefront, they are in a much better position to support and assist each other with individual dreams. They will also be in a much better position to pursue common interests and opportunities. They will actually feel free to dream together because the relationship feels safe and secure again. Only when the "we" priorities are maintained and nurtured will the "me" priorities be embraced and encouraged.

Action Points:

- Agree to stop the painful cycle of tug of war over individual goals and interests.
- Schedule a session with a counselor to determine how to get the focus back on the couple relationship.
- Schedule an extended talk time to collaborate ways of keeping each other's dreams alive and still prioritizing the marriage.
- Plan additional talk times to dream together about shared mission and plans that could include more couple involvement.

LOVE NEEDS

CHAPTER 10

LOVE NEED #10: QUALITY COMMUNICATION

"Seek first to understand and then to be understood."
Stephen Covey

S chedule communication. Everybody knows how to talk but not everybody plans to talk. And not everyone knows how to talk so that it helps their relationship. The couples that do show progress are those that make daily communication an agreed upon priority and put quality "heart talk" on their schedules. Here is our recommendation to couples:

SCHEDULE (and *schedule* is definitely the operative word):
- Daily talk time
- Weekly dates
- Monthly extended times
- Quarterly retreats
- Regular business meetings

Re-read those five statements out loud ? We actually get couples to say those five mandates out loud to each other. We also talk about exactly how to do those activities and put them on calendars. There must be quantity as well as quality talk times together for companions to feel connected and to enjoy each other's company.

How does a couple make their daily talk time more meaningful and of better quality? Let's do a summary of what we teach as the "Speaker-Listener" communication method. In earlier times, Native Americans would gather in a teepee and the chief would hold his "talking stick." The chief would talk first and then when he was finished would pass the stick to another person. Everyone was expected to listen to the one holding the stick. It symbolized "you have the floor" and we need to listen in order to *understand* and not listen in order to *reply*. We have "Native American Talking Sticks" in our offices that we use in this exercise. How do we know that's what they are? Because the tag on the stick says so! And also former Native American clients sent them to us from actual reservations after we had taught them this skill.

Most of the time, instead of using the "talking sticks" we give couples a Kleenex box (safer than a stick!) and write the word "SPEAKER" on the bottom. The skill goes like this: Whoever has the box has the floor and is the designated "speaker." The other partner needs to focus on being the designated "listener." The job of the speaker is to speak for themselves and to speak concisely, giving thoughts, ideas, feelings and requests without any criticism. Always turn your criticism into requests. The job of the listener is to give four responses: *reflect, clarify, explore and validate*. *Reflect* back or paraphrase, "So it sounds like . . ." and mirror back what was heard. *Clarify* by asking, "Is that it. What did I miss?" *Explore* by seeking details. The listener can say, "Explain ___(some part of what was said)___ ." *Validate* by giving some sort of positive feedback to the speaker's ideas and emotions.

How much time is needed on a regular basis in order to grow a healthy relationship? Six hours each week of undistracted devoted couple talk time has been determined to be the "magic" number for master marriages.[1] And these six hours are spread out consistently throughout the week. We recommend couples shoot for 45 minutes every day of media-free speaking and listening together. Have a regular daily time and then add a couple of hours over the weekend. That will be in the right range for effective connection. These daily scheduled times can be enriched with more partner-focused interactions during times of departure, after work reunions, weekly business meetings, affection sharing, date nights, monthly extended times and quarterly retreats.

Action Points:

- Ask your partner to do "Speaker-Listener" and use the Kleenex box to take turns communicating.
- Schedule daily talk times, weekly dates, regular monthly extended times, quarterly retreats and business meetings.
- Interview your partner to determine how to make daily partings and reunions more focused and meaningful.

CHAPTER 11

LOVE NEED #11: CONFLICT MANAGEMENT

"Gentlemen, don't even think about marriage until you have mastered the art of warfare!"
Field Marshal "Monty" Montgomery

When it comes to conflict some people clam up and some people blow up. When feelings get hurt you have to do something with those emotions and they often get *stuffed* or *spewed*. One way to stuff is to act like a turtle. When these folks experience negative emotions they pull into their shells and crawl away from the noise. Others act more like a skunk and spew stink everywhere and on everyone around. And it's amazing how many turtles marry skunks! Have you ever noticed how "fight and flight" often dwell under the same roof creating chaos, conflict and a lot of hurt feelings?

It is good to remember that when you lose your temper you always lose. You lose closeness. You lose peacefulness. You lose trust. You lose safety and security. You lose respect. You can even lose your relationship. When it comes to conflict we should consider the scriptural admonition to "be angry and do not sin; do not let the sun go down on your anger"

49

(Ephesians 4:31). And husbands are exhorted to "love your wives, and *do not be harsh* with them" (Colossians 3:18). Maybe a word to the wise is, "If you keep your mouth shut, you will stay out of trouble" (Proverbs 21:23 NLT). However, one frustrated husband remarked that his favorite verse was, "It is better to live in a corner of the housetop than in a house shared with a quarrelsome wife" (Proverbs 21:9).

It is good to remember that "The Lord's servant must not be quarrelsome" (2 Timothy 2:24). A similar statement is repeated some five times in scripture. The checklist for Christian leadership ranks "not quarrelsome" (1 Timothy 3:3) as a distinguishing character requirement. But everybody has conflict. Every couple has a "fight cycle." *Master Marriages* just do it better and faster than do *Disaster Marriages and with a much better resolution*. So what needs to happen to reduce conflict and increase communication and emotional connection?

Study the following conflict cycle. It usually goes something like this: One person triggers the other and emotions lead to reactions. Reactions lead to triggering the other partner who then experiences emotions with reactions. The trigger-emotion-reaction pattern becomes a predictable rigid negative cycle that can continue indefinitely. Beside each block in the illustration, list your primary triggers, emotions and reactions and ask your partner to list theirs. Then discuss how to improve the cycle.

CONFLICT CYCLE

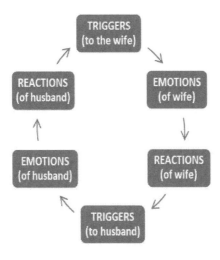

Action Points:

- Study the diagram above separately at first.
- List the triggers (what your partner does) that start conflict for you. Then list the negative emotions that are triggered in you (unloved, neglected, disrespected, , etc.). Next, list your own personal reactions (fight, flight, freeze, criticize, etc.).
- Add to the diagram what your partner records about their triggers, emotions and reactions.
- Discuss ways to reduce (not eliminate) triggers.
- When wounded: Instead of escalating, always call time-out and reschedule ("Ouch. See you in one hour"). The wounded partner should return and share hurt emotions, *not reactions*. The repairing partner must meet emotions with understanding, empathy and apology. See "Chapter 5: Repaired Hurts."

LOVE NEEDS

CHAPTER 12

LOVE NEED #12: BEST FRIEND

"A man that hath friends must show himself friendly."
Proverbs 18:24 KJV

"**I** still love you but I don't like you." That is the statement that we hear so often during counseling sessions. This partner is talking about love vs. friendship. Love is an action verb and friendship takes effort. Friendship can be like a grand butterfly that soars on the wind of everyday positive interactions. The small thoughtful moments of daily life are updrafts or downdrafts that guide friendship.

A couple must develop informal routines of connection in order to be best friends. Spouses send out daily invitations for connection which can be accepted or rejected. These invitations can be either verbal or nonverbal gestures that beckon the other spouse to engage in friendship. These are "bids" for intimacy at an emotional, verbal, relational, spiritual or physical level. The responding partner can either turn toward or turn away from the one inviting. Even the smallest of gestures can determine the landscape and atmosphere of the couple bond.

Each and every invitation is an opportunity to grow

closer or more distant in the overall connection. It is good to discuss and establish new relationship agreements regarding the regular, routine events of the day. Collaborate how to make them more meaningful and relationally connecting. For example, it helps a couple to upgrade the way they depart or return to each other on a daily basis. Instead of yelling "Bye, I'm gone" it would add much more to the friendship bond if you find your partner and depart with a big hug and kiss . . . or at least a hug and a few meaningful words. The same attitude and behavior should apply to every departure and every return home as well as to the many other daily routines in your relationship.

Rethink and upgrade the routines of mealtime, after dinner activities, bedtime, date nights, entertaining at home, vacations, involvement with in-laws, spiritual growth activities, drives in the car and fun times together. Try to be emotionally responsive to even the small, subtle invitations for connection. That is what friends do! Every marital encounter creates a deposit or a withdrawal in the friendship bank which, when compounded determines the overall status of the relationship. What happens on a daily basis significantly affects the friendship factor.

Friends are there for each other. They do things together and they plan to do things together. Find activities that you both could enjoy and even try something new together. The hike up a mountain trail, the first trip to a pottery barn, attending a hockey game or enjoying a concert could do wonders for your friendship. Try going out on weekly dates and take turns surprising each other regarding the place you end up. A few months of that and you will feel like you are on a grand adventure with your best friend.

Friends support each other. No one likes to be criticized. Everyone likes to be appreciated. Every couple needs to create a "mutual admiration society" within the relationship. This can bring great healing for past relationship injuries.

If you think something nice say it twice.

If you see something commendable make sure you compliment it and say it again later for emphasis. The Master Marriages that thrive (not just survive) are the marriages in which partners are in tune with each other's strengths, preferences, backgrounds and daily concerns. It is a powerful predictor of marital friendship when a partner takes time to invest by staying in touch, being involved and showing much affirmation instead of parental-type correction.

Action Points:

1. Evaluate and upgrade your daily routines of connection (e.g., departing and returning home, mealtimes, after meals, bedtimes, weekends, car time, getaways, etc.).

2. Collaborate and schedule activities you could both enjoy. Pick at least three of the following:

- Join me in a favorite activity together (e.g. walking, gardening, working out, etc.)
- Watch a favorite movie or TV program
- Schedule "heart talk" at the end of each day
- Go out with another couple to have fun
- Connect with extended family
- Get take-out dinner and go somewhere different to picnic (a lake, park, etc.)
- Grocery shop and/or cook a meal together
- Invite friends over for an event
- Dream about projects or travel together
- Take a long weekend drive together
- Stop to collaborate whenever needed
- Shop for presents together
- Do spontaneous breakfast, brunch or lunch
- Sit and talk in the morning
- Go out on a special date together
- Get away for the long weekend together
- Participate in a church, ministry, small group or community project together
- Pray together
- Other:_____ .

CHAPTER 13

LOVE NEED #13: RELATIONAL SECURITY

". . . a faithful man who can find?"   Proverbs 20:6b

"I'm never leaving you and if you leave me, I'm going with you!" That's what my wife Rhonda likes to hear and it always seems to bring a smile. Why? Because every spouse wants to know that this relationship bond is "till death do us part." And that is not "till DEBT do us part" like many couples experience!

Every partner wants to know that they will be safe and secure in their primary relationship. Feeling *safe* is mostly about the emotional availability and sensitive responsiveness of one's partner. "Can I trust you with my feelings? Do you care and will you be there for me when I need a refuge?"

Feeling *secure* in the relationship is about longevity and permanence. The questions being asked are, "Can I count on you? Will you ever leave me? Will you ever trade me in for a newer model? Are we going to work through whatever issues come our way or are you going to abandon ship in the next storm? Are you my fair-weather friend or do you want to be my best friend for life?" Couples think about these issues even if they don't talk about them.

Whenever there has been a breach of trust in the couple bond the issue of relational security becomes painfully prominent. Keeping secrets of any kind (time, money, relationships, privacy regarding devices, etc.) can erode the stability of a once secure relationship. And when things get uncovered that have been hidden there is always an immediate "security" breach. Not only will a spouse feel unsafe but they also will feel insecure as though things will not get repaired and continue as before. So the questions arise, "How do I know you will not do this again? And how do I know that you won't give up on us and just leave me behind in the dust and in pain? Are you here to stay? Are you committed to working on and working through whatever we face? Do these recent (and sometime recurring) problems mean that you will be looking for an exit door? Can I count on you to repair the hurts, rebuild the trust and never give up on us?"

Sometimes it is not the offending party about whom long-term relational commitment is questioned. It often becomes the offended person that begins to question their ability or even willingness to continue indefinitely when the offense is great or recurring. We often hear something like, "Your first strike I forgave. With the second strike it became very difficult to forgive. If there is a third strike, you're out. I don't know if I can keep doing this, trying to forgive and move forward unless you really change."

Sometimes we hear a wounded partner say

something like, "Three strikes? How about sixteen strikes?" At some point it becomes too much to bear. If it has become an abusive pattern it should not be tolerated. Repair attempts must include new relationship agreements that demonstrate true, remorse followed by caring and lasting change. Then, and only then, can trust begin to be reestablished. Whoever burned the bridge of trust has to rebuild the bridge of trust. Forgiveness is free but trust has to be earned. And gaining trust takes about three times longer than gaining forgiveness. Many partners are able to forgive within a few months after major offense. But most couples experience one to two years before trust, safety and security are repaired and rebuilt.

Action Points:

- Determine in your heart that marriage is a life-long commitment.
- Remind your partner often that when you said, "I do" you meant "till death do us part." Reassure them, "I do and I always will."
- Be honest with yourself and your partner if you are questioning whether you can keep going on in the relationship. Seek help together from a competent counselor about these issues.
- Ask your partner what makes them feel safe and secure for a lifelong relationship. Then make every effort to take those steps.

LOVE NEEDS

CHAPTER 14

LOVE NEED #14: SHARED DECISION-MAKING

"In essentials, unity; in non-essentials, liberty; in all things, charity."   Saint Augustine

A dominant partner needs to hear, "The two are to become one and YOU ARE NOT THE ONE!" A strong couple bond is forged only when both parties are given a voice and consideration. A good rule of thumb is to, "Let your partner influence you." No one should have the exclusive say-so in a relationship if the relationship is going to be healthy. Consider the other person and their ideas at the same level as you consider your own ideas and preferences. Agree that you will listen in order to understand and not listen in order to reply or react. To work through an important decision (finances, parenting, priorities, purchases, etc.) and build unity in your relationship, complete the following "COLLABORATE" chart.

First, commit to discussing ONE ISSUE and making no decisions to pull any triggers until there is substantial agreement in the middle column. **Secondly**, determine to listen and record both "HER" perspective (ladies go first!) and "HIS" perspective without any negative response or negative body language (sighs, rolling of eyes, etc.). List all possible ideas and consider each other's opinions. Each partner must be willing to hold their preferences with an open hand without demanding their rights or preferences. Otherwise a power struggle will develop. Marriage involves teamwork, not independent unilateral decision-making.

Thirdly, discuss and record any possible ideas or collaborations that could fall into the middle "OUR" agreement column. Seek a "Win-Win," or actually it may look more like an "OK-OK" agreement because it will not be exactly what either partner preferred initially. Determine to quit making "Win-Lose" decisions where one partner gets their way and the other partner feels disregarded. "Win-Lose" decisions always result in the "loser" feeling resentment and eventually even contempt for the other. Then determine a plan (one month experiment) of carrying out the action steps of the "OUR" agreement and plan to reevaluate after the trial period. You can always collaborate again.

COLLABORATE:
#1 Skill for Shared Decision-making

Instructions: Schedule a time to discuss a decision or problem to be solved. **First**, agree to stay focused on one issue only (e.g., parenting, budget, in-laws, savings, etc.). **Secondly**, explain and record the ideas that are "HERS" and then record the ideas that are "HIS." **Thirdly**, seek to find common agreements in the center "OUR" column. Determine to move forward with the "OUR" agreements as a short term experiment (one month). Reevaluate and consider a new collaboration and modification after the initial trial period.

ONE ISSUE: _____

HIS	OUR	HERS

LOVE NEEDS

CHAPTER 15

LOVE NEED #15: SPIRITUAL GROWTH

"If we only spent more time looking at Him we should soon forget ourselves."   D. Martyn Lloyd-Jones

Bill and Martha were a very mature and pleasant middle-aged couple. But something was missing. They had already been to several counselors over a several year period trying to work out the bugs in their marriage. They truly desire to find the connection and unity they once had within their relationship.

We reviewed their relationship history and did not hear of any major traumas or destructive patterns. But when we asked about their spiritual life it became evident where the fracture had occurred. They both had a deeply personal and private faith but it was not something they shared together. We have found that the healthiest and most connected relationships have embraced their longings for the eternal, have come to a sincere faith and following of the Savior and have made a priority of sharing this deep spiritual experience on a regular basis.

We suggested that they start with regular prayer times together. But since there was hesitancy an alternative time of "silent prayer" together was agreed upon. They decided to try this: before going to sleep each night they would hold hands and Bill would lead in silent prayer. He laughed and said, "I think I can do that. Anyone can lead in silent prayer!" So off they went.

They returned a few months later and it was evident that something had improved. The following is what they reported. "We started doing the silent prayer together. Eventually one of us slipped and prayed out loud. Before long we both were praying out loud. Now we are having regular and wonderful times of prayer together." And then they made this jaw dropping statement, "Three months of praying together has done more for our marriage than the previous three years of marriage counseling under three different therapists."

When couples start sharing the deepest, innermost part of who they are there is always a new and profound spiritual connection that transcends typical therapeutic behavioral interventions. Wise King Solomon in 1000 BC understood it. "Unless the Lord builds the house, they labor in vain who build it" (Psalm 127:1). We would say, "God can do more in 5 minutes than we can do in 5 years (or more)."

Spiritual growth in the relationship will involve spiritual leadership, spiritual support and spiritual maturity. Someone needs to step up spiritually and lead in this process of reconnecting vertically with the Lord. We highly recommend this be the husband. And the wife also needs to contribute and participate. Both partners need to turn their primary relational pursuit heavenward and stop expecting their spouse to meet all their relationship needs. Couples that do this together spiritually are the couples that typically move forward relationally with each other.

There are two ways to look at a relationship with the Savior. The Christian life is often viewed as a part-time activity. Christ is accepted as a really good additive but then relegated to being a slice of the pie alongside all the other priorities of life (family, work, church, hobbies, etc.). The way to view a relationship with God is radically different. Christ is not a slice of your priority pie. Christ is at the center like a circle within a circle becoming the hub that affects every part of life. He wants to be the shepherd of your soul and of your relationships. In other words, three months of praying together and sharing this preeminent spiritual relationship could really do more for your marriage than three years of therapy!

Action Points:

- Discuss together the new commitment of surrender to Christ.
- Make the decision together to let God be the first priority in your lives.
- Rethink ways to connect with God (prayer, devotions, church, podcasts, Christian books, worship music, etc.) individually and as a couple.
- Establish regular times of sharing in this adventure.

LOVE NEEDS

CHAPTER 16

LOVE NEED #16: THOUGHTFUL GIFTS

"It is more blessed to give than to receive."   Jesus

Everybody likes presents. But some people like them more than others. One family we know has three daughters. All three daughters were raised with equal love, attention and guidance. At least that is the parents' perspective! But one thing was clearly different. One of the daughters was clearly a "gifts person." No one else in the family responded more to gifts that that daughter. It didn't have to be big gifts . . . just gifts. Hugs didn't bring out the smiles. Time and attention didn't seem all that uplifting. Words of kindness, respect and appreciation were OK. But gifts seemed to light a fire of joy, encouragement and enthusiasm. Some people are just wired that way.

A major part of the celebrations of life such as special days, achievements, birthdays, anniversaries and holidays involve the giving and receiving of gifts. Many families try to teach their children that we all should be more focused on giving than on getting, even though it seems contrary to childish thinking. Receiving a gift brightens the eyes, encourages the hearts and touches the spirits of all children young and old.

Behavioral scientists and theologians continue to

debate what the deepest longings of the human soul may be. The list of longings is enumerated in various forms in countless books and articles. But much of the literature seems to point to three primary needs of the heart. People need value, belongingness and significance. Gifts seem to touch all three of these universal and often unexpressed emotional desires.

Gifts show *value*. Everyone wants to be valued. Everyone likes to feel special. Everyone desires to feel good about themselves. Everyone needs to feel intrinsic worth regardless of performance or success. And an unearned, unrequested gift seems to communicate, "you matter." Gifts bestow a feeling that you are important enough to have someone think of you, consider what you might like, make the effort to go find it and go out of their way to present it to you. This gesture communicates that a person is regarded as existing on Planet Earth for more reasons than to use up air and take up space. It says "you are valuable."

Gifts show *belongingness*. They say, "You matter *to me*. You don't just matter but you matter *to me* as someone that I like or love or both." Presents do say, "I love you" and that "I want to be involved in your life as someone who cares about you." They communicate that the gift-giver is thinking about you, considering your preferences and wanting to reach out to connect with you in a meaningful way.

An appropriate gift can open a door of connection

and relationship. Not only does the receiver of gifts benefit from the giving, the giver also profits. People usually reciprocate warmly to thoughtful gifts. Proverbs 18:16 affirms, "A man's gift makes room for him and brings him before the great."

Gifts also communicate *significance*. They say, "You have accomplished something worth celebrating. You deserve recognition!" Every major (and sometimes minor) achievement deserves recognition. There are three categories of recognition gifts: *personal* gifts, *activity* gifts and *tangible* gifts. Some people respond more to a personal gift-reward such as physical pats on the back, or a verbal "at-a-boy" or "at-a-girl" or "give me a high five." Activity gifts may include, "You did so well that I want to take you on that trip or to that special event/place that you like so much." And of course, we all know what tangible gifts look like. They are simply touchable wrapped up presents that say, "Well done. I'm proud of you and I love you."

Action Points:

- If you especially appreciate gifts make sure you explain this to your partner as a *desire* but not a *demand*.
- If your partner responds exceptionally well to gifts make it a practice to plan ahead and lovingly give gifts that communicate *value*, *belongingness* and *significance*.

LOVE NEEDS

CHAPTER 17

LOVE NEED #17: FINANCIAL AGREEMENT

"Get all you can, save all you can, and give all you can."
John Wesley

There are typically two distinct ways to approach finances as a couple . . . either separately or together. Both options have benefits and both have drawbacks. Often couples are gridlocked and cannot seem to progress toward a mutual agreement about money matters. Rather than polarizing, we recommend a hybrid approach that seems to break that gridlock and create unity.

Separate finances is what one struggling married couple presented in our office. She had her money and he had his. She had her priorities and he had his. She had her friends and he had his. She had her health club and he had his. She had her bedroom and he had his. She had her vacations and he had his. She had her weekend activities and he had his. She had her church and he had his. When asked how their relationship was doing the simultaneous reply was, "Not very good at all." We had to ask, "Are you sure you two are married?" They seemed more like disconnected roommates than two intimate allies. Couples who go down the path of "separateness" are rarely satisfied with the overall results.

Together finances would be at the other end of the continuum. Many couples try to practice this model legalistically and rigidly. They plan together. They budget together. They spend together, or at least try to. They save together. They give together. They reevaluate together. But there tends to be a tension build-up when the focus is always on unity with little or no consideration of autonomy. This is especially true if one partner manages the household finances and the majority of the financial accounts. We have found that healthy satisfied couples give priority to both unity and autonomy. Becoming a unified team is essential but we find an arrangement in which both partners have some personal space, activities and finances consistently grows a better couple bond.

So let's talk about our hybrid model. We recommend that couples take their finances seriously, dedicating both extended times together for planning and regular ongoing "business meetings." And every couple should go through a course to learn about managing money together. We also recommend that couples identify categories as well as personal monthly allowances that are designated to each individual.

One of the biggest breakthroughs we had as a young couple was when Mike woke up to the reality that he was not only managing the money very close to the vest but was also micro-managing what Rhonda was buying at the grocery store each week! It took years before we figured out a better system. It works much better to talk through and agree on a budget for groceries (or whatever the category may be). Then turn that line item or cash amount over to the one who manages that category. When we made that change Mike was less stressed and Rhonda was more encouraged and creative in her role.

For second marriages or later-in-life marriages there are often extenuating financial circumstances that must be considered. Sometimes there are wealth accumulations that were already designated prior to marriage (e.g., retirements, inheritances, college funds, legacy funds, trust funds, etc.). These may need to stay in the sole possession of that partner. Prenuptial agreements are sometimes appropriate in order to protect these vital interests of each partner, their children and their extended family.

Action Points:

- Attend a local course on money management .
- Develop a budget to tell your money where to go.
- Have monthly (or weekly) business meetings to review the finances and collaborate on action items.
- Designate certain line items for each spouse to manage (e.g., groceries, personal spending money, home furnishings, auto repair, etc.). See Chapter 8: Defined Roles and Responsibilities.

LOVE NEEDS

CHAPTER 18

LOVE NEED #18: PHYSICAL ATTRACTIVENESS AND HEALTH

"Behold, you are beautiful my love."   Solomon

When we fall in love we are generally attracted to the total person. However, how they look outwardly is also very important to us. We regularly ask spouses, "Why did you marry this person? What was it that attracted you?" And it is not cool to answer, "I'm still trying to figure that out!" After hearing this question answered more than a thousand times a pattern has emerged.

Our experience shows that couples make the decision to be together for four reasons, in no specific order. Here they are:

1. "The way he/she treated me."
2. "I admired the way he/she was so _____."
3. "I was physically attracted to her/him."
4. "I just knew." Sometimes even, "I felt like God told me."

Physical attractiveness has many facets. Sometimes it is about a face or a figure. Some partners go into elaborate descriptions of this "eye candy" magnetism that was instrumental in bringing the two together.

Others are focused on one aspect of physical attraction like a beautiful smile, buff muscles or a knock-out front side or back side (we have heard it all!). Often the physical attraction is more about the partner's dedication to staying healthy and fit through some form of regular exercise and a healthy diet.

Whatever form is important to each individual, physical attraction is a major part of the overall package that brings couples together. King Solomon was affected by this internal appeal when he stated, "Behold, you are beautiful, my love, behold, you are beautiful!" (Song of Solomon 4:1). He didn't say, "You are a great person and you have such a great personality." He basically said, "You are drop dead gorgeous and you turn me on!" The response he received from his bride was similar, "My beloved is radiant . . ." (Song of Solomon 5:10). She thought he was quite a "hunk!"

Something should be said here about attractiveness in the bedroom. Learning what is and isn't physically attractive in the bedroom is essential for a healthy, growing relationship that avoids stagnation. Bathing, shaving, brushing teeth, grooming, using favorite perfumes/colognes and dressing to please are just a few of the reported personal care aphrodisiacs that reduce mediocrity and stimulate love-making. Take heed to what your partner likes and dislikes. Don't wait until it is too late. See more discussion about this issue in our Chapter 3 on sexual intimacy.

The emphasis on physical attraction doesn't dissipate after the honeymoon. Couples continue to report satisfaction or dissatisfaction with physical appearance over the lifespan of their relationship. Many a spouse sitting on our couch has complimented their partner for taking care of themselves or for looking so nice. And many a partner has complained sadly that their once beautiful or handsome best friend has let themselves due to the lack of effort or self-control. Unfortunately, time and gravity gets us all! But the partners who at least try to maintain (or even improve) their overall health and "good looks" tend to raise the joy and satisfaction level in the couple connection.

Action Points:

- Don't pressure your partner to be something physically that they simply cannot be or do.
- Discuss and set goals to maintain health and fitness individually and together.
- Emphasize the positives, not the negatives (e.g., "your eyes are so pretty" or "you are so strong" or "I love your hair").
- Put emphasis on positive reinforcement for effort (e.g., "way to go") instead of negative comments (e.g., "shame on you").
- Plan some fitness routines together (e.g., walking, biking, going to the gym together weekly, etc.).

LOVE NEEDS

CHAPTER 19

LOVE NEED #19: WORDS OF LOVE

"A word in season, how good it is!"   Proverbs 15:23

"Talk's cheap." That is what many partners will remark in counseling sessions. "I need you to *show* me that you love me. Don't just talk the talk. Walk the walk." But there are some partners who are longing for words of love in addition to the actions of love. Some say that the words of love mean just as much, if not more, than the actions of love.

We often hear, "My parents never said they loved me. I never heard those words growing up." Quite often our clients have had a neglectful or absentee parent with whom they had little or no contact due to work, travel, separation, divorce or death. The result is always a negative imprint from the family-of-origin at best or a deep emotional scar at worst. And this consequence lasts a lifetime. It is a tender wound that seems to easily get reopened in adulthood, and especially by the most significant other.

Many times a primary bread-winner reports that they are gone and working so hard *because* of love. They feel their efforts should be received as love. Then they are bewildered when their labor of love has the opposite effect on their spouse. It seems the more they are gone and focused on outside work, the more the other partner feels unloved and neglected. There is a felt unmet need for more verbal communication of love. And when words of love were lacking from parents in the spouses childhood there is an intensified need for audible affection in the couple relationship.

Sometimes there was a parent who was so stressed and stuck in their own head that they didn't seem to recognize the need of their child for tender words of affection. Sometimes when a partner was growing up their parent or another family member had physical, mental or emotional struggles that demanded extra care-giving. The child was neglected and neglect is actually a form of child abuse. In extreme cases the child might have been forced to step into the adult role to provide the physical and emotional support for the very one who should have been parenting them.

Often the neglectful parents were simply doing what they had seen done as they were growing up. It is not a good excuse but it is an unfortunate family reality for many. Sometimes we hear, "My parents did the best they could with what they had. They did better than their parents did for them so I guess I shouldn't complain." We will agree with part of that statement. We all should be thankful for the good aspects of the parenting we did receive. And maybe some parents were better at being emotionally supportive than their parents had been. But it doesn't remove the imprint of what was lacking. Hopefully this imprint of neglect will not create a permanent "victim mentality" that has excessive control over them. But it does need to be understood by both partners in order to make healthy progress toward emotional bonding as a couple.

There is an aching in the soul of many adults to have some other adult person *speak* sincere words of affection into their life. They are not just looking but also listening for someone who really cares. They want a partner who is not just busy doing loving actions, but one who verbally appreciates their mate. The words may be, "I love you." Or they may be other words of endearment. There are many ways to say as well as show, "I love you." Be creative!

Action Points:

- If this is one of your "Top 10 Love Needs" be sure to explore and discuss *why* words of love mean so much to you.
- Discuss some of the exact phrases that communicate love to you. Is it just, "I love you" or are there other favorite verbal statements that mean a lot to you?
- Read Chapter 6: Respect and Appreciation together.

LOVE NEEDS

CHAPTER 20

LOVE NEED #20: COMFORT AND CARE DURING HARD TMES

"People don't care how much you know, till they know how much you care."   Stephen Covey

A funny interaction takes place in the popular comic strip "Peanuts." Lucy asks Charlie Brown, "Why are we here on earth?" Charlie Brown replies, "To make others happy." She ponders this for a moment and then asks, "Then why are the others here?"

Considering others is the hallmark of Christian virtue. General William Booth, the founder of the Salvation Army, was unable to attend one of their extremely important international conventions because of ill health. So he cabled the delegates a message to be read to all the attendees. The message contained one word in all capital letters: "OTHERS!"

"One another" is one of the most recurring phrases in the Bible. In the original Greek version of the New Testament the word for "one another" is "*allelon*" and it is used exactly 100 times. It is given as a clear imperative 59 of those times for Christians to show concern and love toward others. They were to "be devoted to one another" (Romans 12:10), "care for one another" (1 Corinthians 12:25), "serve one another" (Galatians 5:13), "encourage one another" (Hebrews 10:25), "pray for one another" (James 5:16) and always "love one another" (1 John 4:7). A primary activity of the church was, and still is "one-anothering" one another.

Galatians 6:2 instructs Christians to "bear one another's burdens." A few verses later in that same chapter there seems to be a contradiction when we are told that every person should "bear his own burden" (Galatians 6:5, KJV). So which is it? Should we bear one another's burdens or should we each bear our own burdens? The short answer is both. With close examination of these truths we learn some life lessons.

First, we will all have heavy burdens to bear at times in this life. The burdens mentioned in Galatians 6:2 are burdens of overwhelming situations that could lead us toward a collapse.

Secondly, we should all be ready to help those we love by being there for them when they are going through these extreme circumstances. As one reputable commentator states:

> A serving Christian lends a helping hand with heavy loads (grk. *barē*). This . . . will fulfill the law of Christ, that is, the principle of love (see John 13:34). Though the principle would apply to all burdens, the context (Gal. 6:2) has special reference to the heavy and oppressive weight of

temptation and spiritual failure. The Christian is also instructed to carry his own burden (Gal. 6:5). This does not contradict verse 2 because the reference there is to heavy, crushing, loads (*barē*)—more than a man could carry without help. In this verse (6:5) a different Greek word (*phortion*) is used to designate the pack usually carried by a marching soldier. It is the "burden" Jesus assigns to His followers (cf. Matt. 11:30). There are certain Christian responsibilities or burdens each believer must bear which cannot be shared with others[1]

Each of us has normal life struggles that are burdens for which we should take responsibility. But when the going gets tough and life becomes overwhelming because of personal situations or pressing sins we are people who need people. That is the heart-call of many a partner. "Can I count on you? Will you be there for me when I need you? Will you stand by your man (or woman)?"

Action Points:

- Discuss what situations, trials or temptations are overwhelming in your life both presently and occasionally.
- Explain what care and comfort would look like for you in those situations of struggle.
- Discuss other legitimate available options for care and comfort (e.g., spiritual, relational, encouraging activities, etc.).

LOVE NEEDS

CHAPTER 21

LOVE NEED #21: RECREATIONAL FUN

"God . . . richly provides us with everything to enjoy."
1 Timothy 6:17

"We just don't have fun anymore. We used to do fun things together. But now we are just too busy. We've turned into roommates." These are some of the familiar statements expressed far too often when evaluating distressed couples. The thrill is gone and life has become a pressing routine of endless responsibilities.

King Solomon of Israel is the presumed author of the soul-searching book of Ecclesiastes. The writer was trying to find meaning and purpose in this life. This ancient ruler who was endowed with extreme wealth and wisdom set out to explore and evaluate everything that life and love have to offer. The central theme of his dissertation may be summed up in Ecclesiastes 2:25: "For apart from Him (God), who can eat or who can have enjoyment?" In other words, after trying everything that life and relationships had to offer, he concluded that without God, nothing can fully satisfy.

But with God there is reason to find pleasure and joy in life and relationships. Solomon actually advocates for the enjoyment of life with, "So I commended *pleasure*, for there is nothing good for a man under the sun except to eat and to drink and to *be merry*, and this will stand by him in his toils throughout the days of his life . . ." (Ecclesiastes 8:15, NASB). Scripture is splendidly replete with this wake-up call to remember that God is OK with us enjoying life. "Every good gift and *every perfect gift is from above* [emphasis added], coming down from the Father of lights . . ." (James 1:17). And it is ". . . God, who richly provides us with everything to *enjoy* [emphasis added] " (1 Timothy 6:17).

Jesus, the very Son of God, was far from a kill-joy. Instead He brought encouragement to all when He explained his mission and declared, ". . . I came that they may have *life* and have it *abundantly* [emphasis added]" (John 10:10). He was talking about eternal life in the sweet by and by but He was also talking about an abundant and joyful life in the nasty now and now! Sounds a lot like the admonition, "So if a person lives many years, let him *rejoice* [emphasis added] in them all . . ." (Ecclesiastes 11:8). So how does this all apply to couples and relationships?

"Girls just want to have fun." So go the lyrics of an old pop song. But so do guys. And so do couples. Experiencing common joyful activities is a vital component of any satisfying relationship. When couples talk about the "good ole' days" they usually start recalling special memories of life, love, recreation and fun together (see Chapter 12: Best Friend). We encourage couples to have fresh "dream sessions" now and then. List the things you used to enjoy and the new things you might enjoy now or in the future. Then pick a few and make a plan (see Chapter 14: Shared Decision-Making).

In your dream sessions consider each partner. Things you used to do may not be so enjoyable today. And that is OK. Keep brainstorming. Make a three column worksheet with His, Hers and Our/We activities. Listen to each other and explore with a "no idea is a bad idea" mentality. Just dream together! Eventually you will discover some things that are entertaining or recreational that "We" would like to do. It's all right to give each other permission to do some things alone. Some activities can be done alone or together (e.g., walking, jogging, biking, swimming, movies, special classes, etc.). But make it a point to keep the "We" activities (e.g., special couple events, interests, etc.) just as important as "His" or "Hers" alone activities.

Action Points:

- Have a brainstorming session to list fun and enjoyable activities that could be done together.
- Don't try to start implementing *every* new idea but pick some from the "We" column to start with.
- Do an experiment – try some of the new fun activities and evaluate as you go. You can always make course corrections.

LOVE NEEDS

CHAPTER 22

LOVE NEED #22: REDUCTION OF HARMFUL HABITS

"Catch the foxes for us, the little foxes that spoil the vineyards, for our vineyards are in blossom."
Song of Songs 2:15

B ad habits damage relationships. As marriage counselors we too often hear complaints such as these: "Our worst conflicts are when she has been drinking too much." "He doesn't see anything wrong with smoking a little weed every now and then even though we have children." "I've caught him looking at porn several times and I'm done."

And those last two words, "I'm done" are always hard to hear. We usually respond with, "Is that your final answer?" Sometimes it is and . . . game over. Or at least the session is over. But sometimes the whole relationship is over. Harmful habits take no prisoners if continued. They eventually kill relationships. They create chaos that must be addressed if a couple is to survive and make progress. You can't have a healthy marriage without two healthy individuals. After counseling couples for several decades we have concluded that the *personal and spiritual health* of each individual is the foundational building block for a successful partnership. Marriage counseling often needs to be temporarily suspended if one or both partners are stuck with harmful hurts, habits and hang-ups.

Sometimes we attempt to do both couple therapy and individual counseling. However, this plan is only effective if each individual is making personal changes regarding the hurtful behaviors that have sabotaged the health of the relationship. If one person is hijacking the relationship with addictive practices then couples counseling is counterproductive. One rotten apple (i.e., a really bad habit) starts to ruin the whole batch, so to speak. And the partner who drags the addict into counseling for a marriage miracle is usually disappointed.

These bad habits can run the gamut of everything from unthoughtful mannerisms (e.g., annoying, disruptive, self-focused, inconsiderate behaviors) to all-out sinful, self-harming, impairing, immoral and even criminal addictions. However, sometimes the disruptive partner is repeating behaviors over which they have limited control such as Attention Deficit Hyperactivity Disorder (ADHD), Obsessive Compulsive Disorder (OCD), Anxiety or Depression Mood Disorders. The habits may also stem from the ongoing use of prescribed pain medication due to chronic physical problems. Any of these behaviors can create havoc in a once calm and stable partnership. Life and marriage can get crazy and feel out of control if these behaviors are not halted permanently. One of both persons can be worn so thin that they eventually want to give up.

What is the solution? **Focus on helping the individual more than focusing on helping the relationship.** If you don't fix the personal problems then you will never substantially fix the relationship problems. And how do you fix the personal problems? Find the right resources and experts to address the individual issues. If the harmful behavior is a bent toward inconsiderate narcissism then a skilled pastor or Christian counselor is needed. If it is a chemical/medical issue, then seek out a psychiatrist as well as a counselor for issues like ADHD, OCD, anxiety, depression and pain medication management. If it is a problem with substance abuse or pornography, find a therapist and a support group that specializes in the disruptive pattern. The bottom line is that when harmful behaviors are eroding your relationship, seek out the specialists you need for yourself and for your partner. And don't give up. Stand by your woman (or man) to help them overcome the destructive actions. Then resume the couple relationship therapy.

Action Points:

- Evaluate whether your relationship problems are mostly individual issues.
- Find experienced experts for the individual issues and afterward refocus on relationship repair and rebuilding.

LOVE NEEDS

CHAPTER 23

LOVE NEED #23: TRUST, HONESTY AND INTEGRITY

"Many a man proclaims his own steadfast love, but a faithful man who can find?"   Proverbs 20:6

"**N**o secret keeping." That is the principle we teach couples, and especially when there has been an attachment injury that has created a relationship wound. Trust, honesty and integrity will be at the top of the list of love needs for those who have been hurt because of some inappropriate behavior and/or cover-up. It will typically rank higher than love or commitment for them.

Trust ranks as a significant need for any couple that has experienced a breach of trust. Whenever there has been a deception in the relationship the question will eventually arise, "If they lied about that I wonder what else they might be lying about." Trust is not a luxury. It is a necessity. Without trust you can't move forward. The relationship will lack a sense of safety and security if you are always expecting the next shoe to drop.

Trust and forgiveness are not the same. Forgiveness is a free gift given by one partner to another. It is not accepting or excusing the offense. It is not saying that the offense did not hurt. Forgiveness is also not a feeling. Forgiveness is simply considering the offense and choosing to cut it loose, no longer holding it against the offending partner. From a Christian perspective, forgiveness means turning the offense over to God to let Him deal with the offender (see Romans 12:18-19). Forgiveness is always a *decision* and an *action* followed by a *process*. You have to decide to keep on forgiving after the initial act of releasing the offense and offender to God. Just like with fishing, it is easy to re-snag the same old log and decide to hold on to it for a while. And when you think you have the log snagged, it actually has you snagged. Someone aptly stated, "Unforgiveness is the poison we drink thinking it will kill the other person." It is an acid that destroys the container it is in. You have to let it go and keep letting it go for your sake, for the offender's sake and for the sake of the relationship.

Honesty is supremely important as well. Often a partner will remark, "I am beginning to forgive the offense (e.g., flirting, sexting, porn, drinking, affairs, gambling, etc.) but I don't know if I can forgive the lying and deception." The crime is almost always followed by the cover-up, unfortunately. We often refer to these as twin sins because they almost always go together.

Trust takes time. It usually takes three to four times longer than forgiveness. The forgiveness decision and process is usually moving along pretty well within three to six months for most couples. But rebuilding the bridge of trust usually takes one to two years depending upon the depth of the wound. Whoever burned the bridge of trust has to rebuild the bridge of trust. So how does a couple regain trust after a breakdown of this essential element? We define trust with this simple formula: **Trust = Reassurance + Time**.

Reassurance needs to follow the initial repair work. And what is reassurance? Remember the old grandfather clocks? The big pendulum would swing a few inches to the left and then a few inches to the right. In the case of lying and deception, someone has gone a mile to the left and now they need to go a mile or more to the right to start getting back in balance. In other words, the offending partner needs to give extra effort to make things right again. And that means "no secret keeping" and lots of proactive intentional accountability. No secret activities. No secret people. No secret places. No secret passwords. No secret money. No secret decisions. No secret plans. And once again, the three words to live by: No secret keeping.

Action Points:

- If there is a breach of trust make sure you work through repair attempt conversations. See Chapter 5: Repair Hurts.
- Collaborate on what reassurances are needed to rebuild trust.
- Persevere with the process even if it takes one to two years.

LOVE NEEDS

CHAPTER 24

LOVE NEED #24: PLANNING AHEAD

"Go to the ant, O sluggard; consider her ways, and be wise."   Proverbs 6:6

We are instructed to learn from the and be wise. "Apparently ants have no leader—no commander to direct them, no overseer to inspect their work, no ruler to prod them on . . . Ants also work in anticipation of future needs, storing and gathering while it is warm, before winter comes. The virtue of wisdom is not in being busy but in having a proper view of forthcoming needs that motivate one to action. Those who act only when commanded do not possess wisdom." [1]

Most people want to plan ahead to some degree. Usually one partner is more committed to this than the other. That partner will often experience frustration when little or no attention is given to planning or thinking about the future. There is an interesting passage of scripture that gives instruction about how to care for the members of our households. It states, "But if anyone does not provide for his relatives, and especially for members of his household, he has denied the faith and is worse than an unbeliever" (1 Timothy 5:8). In other words, we should not neglect family.

As was mentioned in Chapter 7: Servant Leader the operative word in that passage is "provide (grk. *pronoeō*)." According to Greek scholar Kenneth Wuest it means "to perceive before, foresee, think of beforehand, provide, to take thought for, care for."[2] The word actually comes from two Greek words; "pro" which means out in front and "noeo" which means to know or think. In other words, it behooves us all to think ahead and plan out in front of where we are presently. We are to be doing that sort of planning not only for ourselves but for all the people entrusted to our care and oversight.

The best place to start is with your spouse and with your immediate family. The faith that we profess verbally should also be professed through our actions by thinking ahead and planning with the purpose of providing for those we love. How can a couple think and plan ahead effectively? As mentioned in previous chapters, we recommend weekly business meetings. Set aside a time once every week (or at least a minimum of twice each month) when the two of you can get away from distractions and discuss the priorities of your family. Plan your priorities, finances, events, parenting and projects together. Early in our marriage we often found ourselves frustrated with each other because we were seldom on the same page about which projects were of highest priority. There were usually dozens of projects to be worked on between the two of us and there was often a tug of war about which was most important. We started using the A-B-C/1-2-3 method of project planning and found that it unified instead of divided us. See this skill in the "Action Points" below.

Consider the ant again. Working together and planning for the future will help you be able to face what lies ahead. But you have to be willing to give some time and attention to this. "The ant is busy throughout the summer, and especially during the harvest, gathering her food for the winter. The point here is that the natural impulse is to care for oneself, to exercise foresight in preparing for the future. Even the humble insects have that much sense."[3] Planning ahead is essential for the growth of a healthy relationship.

Action Points:

- Together make a list of all projects that need attention.
- Together collaborate on which items are A, B or C priority. An A priority means "to be done ASAP." B priority means "to be done after we get the A's done." C priorities can be delayed for now.
- Discuss each A priority and determine A1, A2, etc.
- Schedule the A priorities together on a coordinated calendar.
- At your next business meeting reevaluate your project list and progress.

LOVE NEEDS

CHAPTER 25

LOVE NEED #25: EMOTIONAL AND MENTAL HEALTH

"He that won't be counseled can't be helped."
Benjamin Franklin

W e say it over and over again, "You can't have a healthy relationship without two healthy individuals." If one partner is sick then the focus must be on getting that person healthy again. If one partner is emotionally or mentally overwhelmed with anxiety, depression, grief, trauma or some other debilitating struggle then the attention needs to shift from the overall relationship to the needs of the individual (refer to Chapter 22).

Often there is a trauma that is mucking up the marriage relationship. The trauma may be from a previous relationship such as an associate, an ex-partner or spouse, or even a painful family-of-origin or childhood experience. These past relationship wounds are often more difficult to face. The resistance to process the wound may be unintentional. Personal demons and damages have to be unmasked and explored for them to begin to lose their power over a person. It is always easier to just keep pointing a finger at someone else instead of taking responsibility to deal with the past issues beneath the current issues.

Many times a partner instinctively knows and states, "I'm not ready to work on the marriage relationship until individual issues get resolved." Often they are referring to their partner but sometimes they are referring to their own issues. Occasionally a spouse has practically duct-taped and dragged their partner in by the heels kicking and screaming and propped them up on the counseling couch with a bull-dog determination to get that failure fixed! They have concluded that marriage counseling is the sure-fire fix for everything. But we often recommend pulling back and making the focus more about each individual until each partner is in better position to move forward together. Otherwise everyone gets frustrated.

Some common disorders we see in our office include Mood Disorders, Obsessive-Compulsive Disorder (OCD), Autism Spectrum Disorder (ASD), Attention Deficit Hyperactive Disorder (ADHD), Bi-Polar Disorder (BPD) and Personality Disorders. The fate of a relationship greatly depends on whether each individual is willing to engage in the serious individual therapy when needed. Sometimes this can be accomplished in parallel with marriage counseling but often it means hitting the "marriage-counseling-pause" button until mental and emotional health is established.

Here is a funny but true observation we have made over our years of doing marriage counseling. Most wives eventually decide that their husbands have Narcissistic Personality Disorder and most men come to the conclusion that their overly emotional partner definitely is Bi-Polar or has Borderline Personality Disorder, or both! So maybe every spouse really does have some personal junk to unpack and deal with.

As we discussed in Chapter 22 on "Reducing Harmful Habits" whenever there is substance abuse, inappropriate sexual behaviors, or emotional, verbal or physical abuse you might as well stop the train and let the innocent party off board for a while. Nobody is going anywhere until substantial repair work has been done and change has been implemented as a new-norm lifestyle. Then you can resume with "all aboard" on the love-train of marital therapy.

Action Points:

- Examine together or with an experienced therapist individual issues that may be impeding marital counseling.
- Be willing to delay marital therapy. Seek the appropriate help to explore and work on the personal issues that are affecting you and therefore affecting the couple connection.
- Once there is substantial work being done on the individual issues consider supplementing individual therapy with simultaneous couples therapy.

LOVE NEEDS

CHAPTER 26

LOVE NEED #26: PERSONAL TIME ALONE

"Solitude is the cultivation of serenity."
Chuck Swindoll

Sam was jealous and fearful. All he could think about regarding Sue, his energetic and athletic wife of 20 years, was that she was now spending more time with her girlfriends (and a couple of guy friends) than she was with him. Training for her third triathlon meant early hours in the gym and long hours away from the family on a bike. When she came home she always needed down time. Sue was focused, motivated and professing faithfulness. But Sam was scared and angry. He felt like he was losing her.

Relationships need to be done *together*. Partners need to make time for each other. We have already discussed the essential six hours of weekly, undistracted couple time we refer to as "Heart Talk" (see Chapter 10: Quality Communication). We have talked about other important factors that create and strengthen the couple bond (see Chapter 12: Best Friends and Chapter 21: Recreational Fun). Couples need to think "we" and not just "me" as they do life together. As singles we only had to consider "me." There may have been friends, associates or extended family members that were loosely considered. But none of those relationships required the level of consideration needed to sustain marital oneness. Sue was not considering Sam.

This chapter, however, is not just about the "we" but also the "me" in the relationship. We all need some personal time and space from time to time. All couples need to define what that will look like for them. There is no chapter and verse coming down from heaven to settle this issue. It requires an individualized evaluation and may be more of a reflection of personality needs or overall life situations and, therefore, will fluctuate. This need for personal time may also reflect attachment styles (how the two of you connect differently in relationships). Sam and Sue both had personal interests that needed to be considered.

Some partners enter marriage expecting that things will operate a lot like they did in their single days. The mindset may be, "You go your way, I'll go mine and I'll meet you at home at the end of the day." That would be a lot of attention to "me" and not much focus on "we." Introverts often fall into patterns like that. They get refueled by being alone. So for introverts after a long day at work, with the kids or other activities the couple relationship may even seem taxing since it involves more "people time." At any given moment recharging may be the stronger motivator.

Others mistakenly believe that marriage should be

the death of "me" times and believe it is all about the "we." There may be little or no toleration for individual autonomy. The mentality is that, "Basically we should be joined at the hip and never be apart if we can help it." When that is the prevailing mindset of only one of the partners it tends to put them in the disfavored role of "relationship-police." They press for compliance while the other free-spirited partner feels smothered or caged. We've heard it a thousand times.

Strike a balance. Try not to polarize by thinking that the priority must be mostly "we" or mostly "me." Discuss what each person needs and desires. And realize those needs may change with time and circumstances over the seasons of life. Keep "we" on the center stage of your relationship and weekly planning. But give each other the freedom and blessing to have alone time to pursue individual needs, interests and activities. Healthy relationships breathe and balance the concepts of separateness and togetherness.

Action Points:

- Plan together for "we" activities each week and month.
- Discuss potential "me" time activities and needs. Collaborate and request but don't demand. Consider each other's interests.
- Make it a regular part of weekly "business meetings" to reevaluate.

LOVE NEEDS

CHAPTER 27

LOVE NEED #27: ROMANCE AND PASSION

"Husbands should love their wives . . . nourish and cherish . . ." Ephesians 5:28, 29

*E*ros in Greek Mythology was the god of love, the son of Aphrodite. His Roman equivalent was Cupid, known to us as a cute blind cherub with wings and a bow and arrow. And the word *eros* is also Latin, from Greek, literally meaning "sexual love." But *eros* is more. C. S. Lewis, in his book *The Four Loves*, takes pains in his chapter on *Eros* to make it very clear what *eros* is and isn't. He states,

> By Eros I mean of course that state which we call "being in love" or, if you prefer, that kind of love which lovers are "in." It is the love that is least thought about but most felt. It is sexual and not. It seeks one and only one person. Eros makes a man really want, not a woman, but one particular woman. In some mysterious but quite indisputable fashion the lover desires the "beloved" herself, not the pleasure she can give. The fact that she is a woman is far less important than the fact that she is specifically herself. This love does not aim at happiness, but on a particular person. Better to be miserable with her than happy without her. Can we be in this selfless liberation for a lifetime? Hardly

for a week. Between the best possible lovers this high condition is intermittent. So what are we to do? We must do the works of Eros when Eros is not present. This all good lovers know.[1]

Romance and passion often include a state of mind known in present psychological vernacular as "limerence." It is has been described as "an involuntary interpersonal state that involves an acute longing for emotional reciprocation characterized by obsessive-compulsive thoughts, feelings, and behaviors, and emotional dependence on another person."[2] The physiological features of intense limerence can include seizure-like trembling, pallor, flushing, awkwardness, stuttering, shyness, confusion, heart palpitations, pupil dilation and even general weakness. Less common effects include insomnia, loss of appetite and sometimes passing out.

Some call limerence infatuation, lovesickness, a crush, or romantic love, while others relate it to love addiction. Some have humorously called it "affection deficit disorder" since the intense desire can turn to despair when met with an unequal or even unrequited love response.

Much to the dismay of diehard romantics, research suggests that "limerence is the result of biochemical processes in the brain. Responding to cues from the hypothalamus, the pituitary gland releases norepinephrine, dopamine, phenyl ethylamine (a natural amphetamine), estrogen and testosterone. This chemical cocktail produces the euphoria of new love and begins to normalize as the attachment hormones (vasopressin and oxytocin) kick in, typically six to 24 months into a relationship."[3]

Romance and passion may come and go. But one thing is certain – feelings follow behavior. When partners engage in caring, loving, kind and thoughtful behaviors the feelings of love and romance tend to emerge. *Eros* is not the engine for the love-train. *Eros* is more like the dining car or maybe even the caboose. It comes along for the ride and brings much joy and pleasure. But it cannot be expected to lead the journey. C. S. Lewis was right. We must do the works of *eros* even when *eros* is not present.

Action Points:

- Discuss this chapter with your partner to give new perspectives on romance and passion.
- Discuss what romance and passion look like for each of you at this season of your relationship.
- Make plans to be more intentional and proactive with this new understanding of what your partner likes and wants.
- Consider adjustments to your expectations and behaviors.

LOVE NEEDS

CHAPTER 28

LOVE NEED #28: CONNECTION WITH FRIENDS AND FAMILY

"A man who has friends must himself be friendly . . . "
Proverbs 18:24 (NKJV)

Mike's mom used to say, "The Bible may say *leave and cleave* but it doesn't say *desert and hurt*!" Good point. The context of that admonition was usually when we were home for the holidays and she had been missing us and her grandchildren. Moms can be quick to remind us about that sort of thing!

Sometimes in a couple relationship one partner is all about going to see the relatives over and over and over again (did I mention "over"?). It is often that same partner who is filling up the social calendar saying, "I miss my friends and I wish we could spend more time with them. When can we go see .them?" It is always quite amazing how so often a life-of-the-party raging extrovert ends up with a quiet, home-body introvert. Go figure! It happens. Opposites attract but opposites can also attack! The very enchanting qualities that drew us together can eventually get on our last nerve and push us apart.

Connecting with family and friends can be a

grandmother's request. But it is often a partner's request to the other partner. Frequently one partner has close ties with parents and other extended family members that may be the result of positive early experiences. When a single parent or grandparent has raised a child there is often an endearing connection with that child. Parent-child bonds are real. Remember Elvis bought his mother a Cadillac!

Looking out for our aging parents or in-laws isn't wrong. There may be seasons where that is even the focus. It is actually a clear biblical injunction to care: "But if any widow has children or grandchildren, let them first learn to show piety at home and to repay their parents; for this is good and acceptable before God" (1 Timothy 5:4, NKJV). But there are some situations that have negative aspects that need to be screened and corrected.

A certain kind of dysfunctional family-of-origin can create lingering push-pull dynamics from which it is difficult to extract oneself. Beware of a controlling or manipulative parent, a parent who can't let go, or a struggling or dependent parent. A closed family system that doesn't allow for growth and change is unhealthy, as is a mother-in-law who is never satisfied, or adult siblings who still dictate extended family priorities. Don't let an enmeshed, dysfunctional family-of-origin place your current couple relationship in jeopardy.

Sometimes the desire and request of one partner is

to connect regularly with non-family friends. Often we hear about "girls' night out" or "guy time." Gathering with hunting and fishing buddies, church or school friends, game night pals, and good 'ole neighborhood cookouts are regular calendar highlights for many couples. In addition, planning and attending special events with workplace "family" has become the new relationship circle for many.

Nonetheless, it is usually the more relational partner that tends to drive the social agenda and can easily frustrate the less relational partner. Be sensitive. Don't keep pushing and pressuring each other. If you are the less social spouse be willing to consider some of the high social interests of your mate. Whoever has more physical energy should not expect the other person to come up to their level of activity. Even if they do come up to that level of output for a while, they will not be able to sustain it and will begin to resist any requesting or coaxing. Find a balance that you both can live with and make that your new social norm.

Action Points:

- Be willing to hear and make concessions over your partner's request for more or less involvement with family and friends.
- See Chapter 14: Shared Decision-making, and collaborate over social activities. Make an effort to meet in the middle.

LOVE NEEDS

CHAPTER 29

LOVE NEED #29: UNITED PARENTING

"Few men and women will ever do anything more important than nurturing and raising the next generation." James Dobson

I n his landmark parenting book, *Dare To Discipline*, Dr. James Dobson popularized the "tough love" and "tender love" parenting styles. He explained how to balance gentle, affirming love with values-based discipline through common sense child-rearing. Scripture states, "Do not provoke your children to anger, but bring them up in the discipline (grk. *paideia*) and instruction (grk. *nouthesia*) of the Lord" (Ephesians 6:4). Discipline refers to the training and correction of tough love. Instruction is the encouragement and exhortation of tender love. Dobson promoted the *law of reinforcement* to instill positive behaviors and change negative behaviors. He stated, "The parent-child relationship is the first and most important social interaction a youngster will have."[1]

Spouses don't always see eye to eye on these issues. But parents should come together. Children need their parents to show up in a big way to provide the tough and tender love they desperately seek. The following is a summary of evidence-based research on the basic elements that could result in successful parenting: responsiveness vs. unresponsiveness and demanding vs. undemanding.[2] Building on those ideas, four parenting styles emerge:

Authoritative (Strong): This parent is demanding and responsive. They are both tough and tender. Most studies have shown that children with authoritative parents have the best outcomes in many different areas. This type of parenting with parental support, strong monitoring and firm boundaries is linked to higher grades and better overall performance academically and socially.[3]

Authoritarian (Demanding): This parent is demanding but not responsive. They are extremely tough without being tender. Their parenting is restrictive, punishment-heavy with little or no explanation to the child. The "helicopter parent" is a variation of this style. The goal of this parent, at least when well-intentioned, is to teach the child to behave, survive, and thrive in an unforgiving, cruel world. This degree of toughness has distinctive negative effects on children. They will have less social competence because they are used to being told what to do. They tend to be conformists, highly obedient and quiet, but not very happy. They often suffer from depression, eventually rebel, and are at high risk for self-blame and escapist behaviors such as substance abuse and suicide.[4]

Permissive (Indulgent): This parent is responsive and not demanding. They are mostly tender with little or

no toughness. This style is characterized as having few expectations, demands or controls over the children. This is total child-centered parenting with the parent taking on the role of friend. Indulgent parents do not require children to regulate themselves or to behave appropriately. The outcome studies show that these children stay immature, lack impulse-control, tend to be irresponsible and engage in misconduct because they expect to get their way.[5]

Neglectful: This parent is undemanding and unresponsive. They are neither tough nor tender. This is the parent who has checked out with little or no interest or availability to the child. They have made something else a priority and basically left the child to raise himself. "The authoritarian style doubles the risk of bad behavior but research shows the neglectful parent triples the chance of a child acting out even with criminal behavior."[6]

Action Points:

- Study the four parenting styles above together and humbly identify which one you each tend to follow.
- Rethink parenting and consider how you could implement the Authoritative/Strong style together.
- Avoid using two extreme styles, trying to counterbalance what your spouse is doing. (Good cop/Bad cop syndrome).

LOVE NEEDS

CHAPTER 30

LOVE NEED #30: SUPPORTIVE HELP

Do all the good you can, by all the means you can, in all the ways you can, in all the places you can, at all the times you can, to all the people you can, as long as ever you can." John Wesley

The day began at 0 dark 30 for Bob, Jill and the kids. In fact, every day seems to start in a stressful panic with alarms going off and kids resisting the morning routine. Mom and Dad are rushing through the bathrooms and running back and forth to make sure the kids are getting ready. The kids are mumbling something about wanting to stay home and what they forgot to complete for that one teacher. The parents grab cups of coffee and armloads of stuff as they head off for carpool and work and a dozen priorities for the day. The day is a blur. And when the first spouse gets home pandemonium resurfaces during the after school bewitching hours. While tending to supper, supervising the kids' homework and sorting out the battles of the day the busyness continues. And then – in walks the other adult partner ready to check out, turn on the television and chill. Can we say tension?

What if we could hit the pause button and rewind the video back to the Sunday night before when the couple had their regularly scheduled weekly business meeting to plan the priorities and activities of the week? Or does that sound like too much of a fairy tale? Maybe you should stop right here and go back and reread Chapter 14: Shared Decision-Making and Chapter 24: Planning Ahead. Some preemptive decisions could have been forged together at the weekly business meeting before the chaos ensued.

Don't wait until you are in the midst of the daily battles. It's practically too late for many couples by then. Sit down and determine who will be doing what each day. Think through the daily routines and how you can work together to manage the high tides of stressors and responsibilities. Come up with agreements on how to help each other during the week. The couples who fail to plan, plan to fail. But the couples who face the foe of feeling overwhelmed and under-supported can usually emerge victors and teammates by planning.

For example, one couple with little children created a strategy that became a game-changer and a life-saver, after the goading of their therapist. The overstressed stock-broker dad decided to be more disciplined about leaving the office at a regular, agreed upon hour (he could have easily stayed much later every night). And because of all the high pressure he faced every day he determined to stop on his way home at a certain city park where he could decompress. By doing this he was able to clarify the greatest monster deals that would be clawing for his attention when he returned the next day. He also made it a habit of putting all of his worries and cares in a lock-box (his briefcase) and relax a few minutes while listening to a few favorites from his vast collection of Johnny Cash's greatest hits.

After that he was able to don his cape and activate super powers. "Tah-dah!" When he got home he could then emerge as "Super-Husband" and " Super-Dad," fully equipped to swoop in and begin helping his wife with the evening tasks! After this new protocol for reentry was implemented a whole new marriage and family emerged. The bedraggled wife found herself uplifted and much more encouraged about their evenings together. The kids, who were usually swinging from the chandeliers and wreaking havoc on several rooms, began to learn calmness and guidance from an engaged father. This husband was learning personal self-control in order to practice a servant's heart toward those he truly loved. The great outcomes continue to this day.

Action Points:

- Establish a weekly couple's business meeting and make the division of roles and responsibilities a key agenda item.
- Troubleshoot and tackle the hot spots of the week and what needs to happen to share the load of home and family.

LOVE NEEDS

Endnotes

Introduction:
"Blaise Pascal Quotes About Jesus;" available from
https://www.azquotes.com/author/11361-Blaise_Pascal;
accessed 15 August 2018.
[2] Elizabeth Barrett Browning, *Sonnets from the Portuguese and other Love Poems* (New York: Doubleday, Reissue 1990), 6-7.

Chapter 1: Love Need #1 - Working on Our Relationship
"Millennials: A Portrait of Generation Next;" available from
http://www.pewsocialtrends.org/files/2010/10/millennials;
accessed 20 September 2017.

Chapter 2: Love Need #2 - Emotional Closeness
Tim Clinton and Sharon Hart Morris, *Why You Do The Things You Do* (Nashville: Thomas Nelson, 2006), 178.
[2] John Gottman, *The Relationship Cure* (New York: Crown, 2001).

Chapter 3: Love Need #3 - Sexual Intimacy
Shere Hite, *The New Hite Report* (New York: Seven Stories Press, 2003).

Chapter 4: Love Need #4 – Physical Connection
Ruth Feldman, Zehava Rosenthal, Arthur Eidelman, *"Maternal-Preterm Skin-to-Skin Contact,"* Biological Psychiatry 75 (1) (2014):56.

Chapter 6: Love Need #6 – Respect and Appreciation
Emerson Eggerichs, *Love and Respect* (Brentwood: Integrity, 2004), 16.
[2] John Gottman and Julie Gottman, *Bridging The Couple Chasm: Level 1* (Seattle: The Gottman Institute, 2014), 1.22-23.

Chapter 7: Love Need #7 – Servant Leader
Spiros Zodhiates, *The Complete Word Study Dictionary: New Testament.*

Chapter 10: Love Need #10 – Quality Communication
John Gottman, *The Seven Principles for Making Marriage Work* (New York: Harmony Books, 2015), 277-278.

Chapter 20: Love Need #20 – Comfort and Care During Hard Times

D. K. Campbell, *Galatians.* In J. F. Walvoord and R. B. Zuck (Eds.), *The Bible Knowledge Commentary: An Exposition of the Scriptures* (Wheaton: Victor Books, 1985), 609-610.

Chapter 24: Love Need #24 – Planning Ahead

S.S. Buzzell, *Proverbs.* In J.F. Walvoord & R. B. Zuck (Eds.), *The Bible Knowledge Commentary: An Exposition of the Scriptures* (Wheaton: Victor Books, 1985), Vol. 1, 916.

[2] K. S. Wuest, *Wuest's Word Studies From the Greek New Testament* (Grand Rapids: Eerdmans, 1997).

[3] J. E. Smith, *The Wisdom Literature and Psalms* (Joplin: College Press Pub. Co., 1996).

Chapter 27: Love Need #27 – Romance and Passion

C. S. Lewis, *The Four Loves* (New York: Harcourt Brace, 1960), 117-149.

[2] Dorothy Tennov. *Love and Limerence: The Experience of Being In Love* (Lanham: Scarborough House, 1998), 17.

[3] David Sack, M.D., *Limerence and the Biochemical Roots of Love Addiction*," Huffington Post; available from https://www.huffingtonpost.com/david-sack-md/limerence; accessed February 24, 2018.

Chapter 29: Love Need #29 – United Parenting

James Dobson, *Dare To Discipline* (New York: Bantam Books, 1977), 17.

[2] Diana Baumrind, "Child care practices anteceding three patterns of preschool behavior," *Genetic Psychology Monographs*, no. 75 (1967):43-88.

[3] Paul Amato and Frieda Fowler, "Parenting Practices, Child Adjustment, and Family Diversity," *Journal of Marriage and Family*, 64 (3) (2002):703.

[4] Kathleen Stassen Berger, *The Developing Person Through the Lifespan* (New York: Worth Publishers, 2011), 274.

[5] Sanford Dombusch, Philip Ritter, P. Leiderman, Donald Robert, and Michael Fraleigh, "The Relation of Parenting Style to Adolescent School Performance," *Child Development* (1987): 58.

[6] Amanda Verzello, "Teens and alcohol study: Parenting Style Can Prevent Binge Drinking;" available from https://news.byu.edu/news/teens-and-alcohol-study-parenting-style-can-prevent-binge-drinking; accessed March 14, 2018.

Love Needs Assessment
Discover Your
"Top 10 Love Needs"

INSTRUCTIONS: Consider each of the Love Needs below. Evaluate the importance of each one as a felt need for you to receive from your partner *at this present time*. Circle your corresponding rating from 1-7 (with 7 being high). After ranking all 30 items, place a check (√) to the right beside your top 10 highest scores. Then rank your top 10 in order of priority on the last page.

Love Needs   **Importance**   **Top 10 (√)**

1. Working on our relationship (making it a priority)
   1 2 3 4 5 6 7   _____
2. Emotional closeness (feeling connected and close)
   1 2 3 4 5 6 7   _____
3. Sexual intimacy (quality and frequency)
   1 2 3 4 5 6 7   _____
4. Physical connection (touching, hugging, cuddling)
   1 2 3 4 5 6 7   _____
5. Repaired hurts (healing our personal relationship injuries)   1 2 3 4 5 6 7   _____
6. Respect and appreciation (words and/or actions that validate)   1 2 3 4 5 6 7   _____
7. Servant leader (considering me and my needs)
   1 2 3 4 5 6 7   _____
8. Defined roles and responsibilities (agreeing on division of labor)   1 2 3 4 5 6 7   _____
9. Support my desire to help others (being positive about my efforts)   1 2 3 4 5 6 7   _____

10. Quality communication (consistent positive talk time)

    1 2 3 4 5 6 7   _____

11. Conflict management (working through our issues together)   1 2 3 4 5 6 7   _____

12. Best friend (being together and doing things together)

    1 2 3 4 5 6 7   _____

13. Relational security (reassurance of our future together)

    1 2 3 4 5 6 7   _____

14. Shared decision-making (mutual respect in collaboration)

    1 2 3 4 5 6 7   _____

15. Spiritual growth (individually and together)

    1 2 3 4 5 6 7   _____

16. Thoughtful gifts (small or large tokens of love)

    1 2 3 4 5 6 7   _____

17. Financial agreement (determining our goals and following a plan)   1 2 3 4 5 6 7   _____

18. Physical attractiveness & health (staying fit and healthy)

    1 2 3 4 5 6 7   _____

19. Words of love (loving and affirming statements to me)

    1 2 3 4 5 6 7   _____

20. Comfort and care during hard times ("being there" for me)   1 2 3 4 5 6 7   _____

21. Recreational fun (having fun and playing together)

    1 2 3 4 5 6 7   _____

22. Reduction of harmful habits (irritations, addictions, etc.)

    1 2 3 4 5 6 7   _____

23. Trust, honesty and integrity (demonstrating trustworthiness)   1 2 3 4 5 6 7   _____

24. Planning ahead (our priorities, goals and calendar)

    1 2 3 4 5 6 7   _____

Importance   Top 10 ($\sqrt{}$)

25. Emotional and mental health (progress on individual
    issues)   1 2 3 4 5 6 7   _____

26. Personal alone time (supporting my "me" time)
                                   1 2 3 4 5 6 7   _____

27. Romance and passion (proactively pursuing me)
                                   1 2 3 4 5 6 7   _____

28. Connection with friends and/or family (involved with
    loved ones)   1 2 3 4 5 6 7   _____

29. United parenting (functioning as a team with each child)
                                   1 2 3 4 5 6 7   _____

30. Supportive help (volunteering to lift my personal load at
    times)   1 2 3 4 5 6 7   _____

**After completion of this assessment, rank (in order)
your "Top 10 Love Needs" on the next page.**

My Personal "Top 10 Love Needs"

<u>Instructions:</u> Review your scores on the "Love Needs Assessment." On this worksheet, rank/prioritize the "Top 10 Love Needs" that you personally selected . Write some practical examples beside each one. Take extended time to discuss these with your partner and learn their "Top 10 Love Needs" with examples. Take notes in the back of this book.

1st: _____

2nd: _____

3rd: _____

4th: _____

5th: _____

6th: _____

7th: _____

8th: _____

9th: _____

10th: _____

<u>FOLLOW-UP</u>: Transfer your personal "Top 10 Love Needs" (with examples) to an index card and trade cards with your partner. Review these cards daily for one month (and periodically) to be more effective at giving and receiving love. Retake this Love Needs Assessment annually since felt needs tend to change over time and seasons of life.

LOVE NEEDS

LOVE NEEDS

56176595R00083

Made in the USA
Columbia, SC
24 April 2019